YOUNG JEAN LEE is a playwright, director, and filmmaker who has been called "the most adventurous downtown playwright of her generation" by the *New York Times* and "one of the best experimental playwrights in America" by *Time Out New York*. She became the first Asian-American woman to have her play produced on Broadway with *Straight White Men*. She has written and directed ten shows in New York with Young Jean Lee's Theater Company. Her plays have been performed in more than eighty cities around the world and have been published by Dramatists Play Service, Samuel French, Theatre Communications Group, and Nick Hern Books. Her short films have been presented at The Locarno International Film Festival, Sundance Film Festival, and BAMcinemaFest. Lee is the recipient of a Guggenheim Fellowship, two OBIE Awards, a Prize in Literature from the American Academy of Arts and Letters, a PEN Literary Award, a United States Artists Fellowship, a Doris Duke Performing Artist Award, a Foundation for Contemporary Arts grant, an Edwin Booth award, the ZKB Patronage Prize of the Zürcher Theater Spektakel, and the Windham-Campbell Prize.

UNTITLED FEMINIST SHOW

STRAIGHT WHITE MEN

Young
Jean
Lee

NICK HERN BOOKS
London
www.nickhernbooks.co.uk

A Nick Hern Book

Straight White Men & Untitled Feminist Show first published in Great
Britain in 2021 as a paperback original by Nick Hern Books Limited,
The Glasshouse, 49a Goldhawk Road, London W12 8QP, by special
arrangement with Theatre Communications Group, Inc., New York

"Peter Piper" by Joseph Ward Simmons and Darryl McDaniels © 1986
Arista Records LLC. *The Birth of Tragedy: Out of the Spirit of Music*,
by Friedrich Nietzsche (1872), Shaun Whiteside, translator, Penguin
Classics, London, 1993. The author thanks the Rodgers & Hammerstein
Organization for its kind cooperation with the author's parody of the song
"Oklahoma" as used in *Straight White Men*.

Cover design by Mark Melnick

Designed and typeset by Lisa Govan for Theatre Communications Group,
Inc.

Printed in the UK by Mimeo Ltd, Huntingdon, Cambridgeshire PE29 6XX

A CIP catalogue record for this book is available from the British Library

ISBN 978 1 83904 053 5

CAUTION   All rights whatsoever in these plays are strictly reserved.
Requests to reproduce the texts in whole or in part should be addressed to
the publisher.

Performing Rights   Applications for performance, including readings
and excerpts, by amateurs and professionals should be addressed to Olivier
Sultan, CAA, 405 Lexington Avenue, 19th Floor, New York, NY 10174,
email olivier.sultan@caa.com, *tel.* (212) 277.9000

No performance of any kind may be given unless a licence has been
obtained. Applications should be made before rehearsals begin. Publication
of these plays does not necessarily indicate their availability for amateur
performance.

FOR
LEE SUNDAY EVANS,
MORGAN GOULD,
EMILYN KOWALESKI,
AND
LEAH NANAKO WINKLER

UNTITLED FEMINIST SHOW

FOR CALEB HAMMONS

PRODUCTION HISTORY

Untitled Feminist Show premiered at the Walker Art Center in Minneapolis on January 5, 2012. It was performed by:

World Famous *BOB*	PERFORMER 1
Becca Blackwell	PERFORMER 2
Amelia Zirin-Brown (Aka Lady Rizo)	PERFORMER 3
Hilary Clark	DANCER 1
Regina [Sic]	DANCER 2
Katy Pyle	DANCER 3

Conceived and directed by Young Jean Lee in collaboration with Faye Driscoll, Morgan Gould, and the original performers. Associate director, Morgan Gould. Produced by Aaron Rosenblum. Dramaturgy by Mike Farry. Set design by David Evans Morris. Sound design by Chris Giarmo and Jamie McElhinney. Lighting design by Raquel Davis. Video design by Leah Gelpe. Associate video design by Bart Cortright. Associate lighting design by Ryan Seelig. Production supervisor, Sunny Stapleton.

Special thanks to Caleb Hammons and Bianca Leigh, who were part of the show's initial development, and to Malinda Ray Allen, Desiree Burch, Cynthia Hopkins, Madison Krekel, Erin Markey, and Jen Rosenblit, who performed in tours of the show.

Additional thanks to Jennifer Devere Brody, Joshua Bastian Cole, Melanie LaBarge, Frances Lee, Amani Starnes, and Sista Zai Zanda, my intersectional feminist/gender theory consultants for the published script; as well as to Emilyn Kowaleski, who took a first pass at documenting the movement; and to Andrew Hoepfner, who wrote most of the descriptions of the original production's sound. Thanks also to the countless other people who collaborated on the text for this script.

Untitled Feminist Show was originally commissioned by the Walker Art Center, and is a co-production of the Walker Art Center, steirischer herbst, Kunstenfestivaldesartes, the Spalding Gray Award (PS122 New York, Warhol Museum Pittsburgh, On the Boards Seattle), and Young Jean Lee's Theater Company (Young Jean Lee, Artistic Director; Aaron Rosenblum, Producing Director).

The show was remounted at the Baryshnikov Arts Center in New York City, with the same cast and production team. It opened on January 15, 2012.

This show was created by a group of American feminists, and whenever the word "feminist" appears, it refers to feminism as seen through our particular cultural lenses. Moreover, *Untitled Feminist Show* isn't a show *about* feminism. It doesn't attempt to explain feminism or say anything new about it. Rather, as the title indicates, this is a feminist show.

I made this show in collaboration with choreographer Faye Driscoll, associate director Morgan Gould, and performers Becca Blackwell, Hilary Clark, Katy Pyle, Regina [sic], Amelia Zirin-Brown (aka Lady Rizo), and World Famous *BOB*. My collaborators and I focused on one aspect of feminism: the exploration and creation of gender-fluid spaces where people are free to express themselves without regard for the rules of the male/female gender binary. We wanted to create a fantasy world in which people—regardless of what gender they were assigned at birth—could embody a range of identities without being shamed or discriminated against.

To many of the show's creators, the idea of a gender-fluid world seemed appealing, because we felt oppressed by the gender labels assigned to us. However, we realize this isn't the case for everyone, and the show doesn't mean to suggest that everyone should identify as gender fluid. Rather, the show is a demonstration of the *potential* for gender fluidity within the human form.

This show was created out of the experiences of people who had, at some point in our lives, been perceived as women or girls, whether we chose this or not. Therefore, the roles were designed for people like us to perform. However, the absence of parts for cisgender (cis) men—that is, men whose gender corresponds to their birth sex—isn't meant to suggest that we believe cis men should be excluded from the creation of a gender-fluid world.

The performers should be completely nude throughout the entirety of the show, since any trace of clothing or decoration inevitably marks them as "feminine" or "masculine" to the audience. Hairstyling and makeup (including foundation and nail polish) shouldn't be used, for the same reason, and also to empower the performers to be fabulous as they are. Prosthetics are fine as long as the performer uses them in daily life and/or considers them a part of their body.

Untitled Feminist Show isn't meant to be an intellectual experience. It uses the language of movement to generate emotion in the audience. Therefore, with the exception of the recorded pre-show announcement and the song in Welsh, there should ideally be no words or lyrics (live or recorded) in the show, whether spoken, projected, played, or sung. With that said, in our production we did include a few background words and phrases in some of our music tracks, but they were either incomprehensible or relatively meaningless.

Because the performers' bodies should do as much of the communicating as possible, frilly pink parasols are the only props. Note: The color pink has been critiqued as a symbol of exclusionary white feminism. I think this is unfortunate, as this view can easily align with the long history of misogyny already attached to the color ("wearing pink makes you weak like a girl or gay"). This show treats pink parasols as symbols of historically despised "femininity," rather than symbols of feminism or of women as a whole. Feel free to replace them with whatever symbol of "femininity" you'd like.

This show doesn't subscribe to the view that performance art should be aggressive toward and destructive of all that came before it. It doesn't scorn conventionally pleasing choreography, prettiness, or childishness. It wasn't made to provide a sense of boundary-pushing novelty for highly educated sophisticates.

Rather, the purpose of *Untitled Feminist Show* is to create joy. It is meant to be an act of generosity and love.

The scene headings and statements of purpose are strictly for the production team and performers. They are not meant to be printed in the program, heavily signaled via the choreography, or otherwise banged over the audience's heads. For most of the scenes, it's great if the audience has no idea what's happening intellectually. The intention is to engage people emotionally.

I've included some diagrams from the original production as a visual reference. Unless otherwise indicated, the diagrams show the performers' positions from above (with the audience at the bottom of the drawings). They are not meant to be prescriptive, so feel free to ignore them.

The production team and cast should be as diverse as possible. To that end, it's important that the performers represent a range of body types. There are six performers in the show, three of whom must be skilled dancers. The performers playing Performer 1 and Dancer 1 should be full-figured/people of size. Performer 1 should have a female-coded body, in the sense that they must have breasts (or a breast) and a vagina (but it doesn't matter if they were born with them or not). Dancer 1 should have long hair and a female-coded body. The performer playing Performer 2 should be a transgender person who is a good actor. The performer playing Dancer 2 should identify as female and be able to sing badly. Performer 3 should have a female-coded body, be able to do a handstand, and be a good singer and comedian. Dancer 3 should identify as female and be able to do a handstand and to lift Dancer 2. It's helpful if Dancer 3 can be dance captain.

When the word "PERFORMERS" appears in all-caps, it refers specifically to the performers rather than the dancers. When "performers" appears in lowercase letters, it refers to both performers and dancers.

This script uses the singular pronoun "they" for all of the characters, without regard to the real-life gender identifications of the performers. However, each production is encouraged to choose (or invent) their own gender-free pronoun(s) to use when discussing the characters.

Performers, if a member of the production team is taking the show in a direction that you feel is antithetical to the spirit of the show, please speak up. Production team, please make an effort to cast people whom you trust to communicate in open and productive ways. I recommend that you have a conversation with anyone whom you're interested in casting before you cast them.

The sound design is essentially the "text" for the piece and will require a significant investment of time and energy. Feel free to experiment with a multitude of instruments, sampling, field recordings, and both electronic and acoustic elements. Some iterations of this show might even work with live musicians. The ultimate goal is to accommodate the needs, musically, of each section of the piece. Therefore, having a broad range of musical options available is important. For the original production, we had two sound designers working in tandem, one of whom was a deejay. I've included detailed descriptions of the original sound design in order to emphasize the detail and specificity required, but you should feel free to ignore these and do whatever best serves the needs of your show.

Although I regard this as a theater piece rather than a dance piece, it is physically very challenging to perform—more so than many dance pieces. It should be rehearsed and performed on a proper dance floor. For our production, the emphasis on symmetry required performers to repeatedly work one side of their bodies and not the other. Make room in your budget for massage or other physical therapies to prevent injury.

Performing the show requires a huge amount of physical, emotional, and spiritual energy, much of which the performers receive from each other. Try to find performers who are easy to get along with and confident in their ability to do this particular show. Insecurity and interpersonal tension are deadly to the show's effectiveness.

If you haven't worked with nudity before, here are some common-sense tips that I wish someone had given me before I started. Rehearse clothed whenever possible. We used nude-colored clothing for most of our tech rehearsals.

When performers are nude, make sure you can control the temperature in the room and prevent outsiders from walking in, and have a lot of baby wipes on hand. Performers should avoid applying body lotion before going onstage—it can get on the floor and create a slipping hazard.

For some transgender performers, being nude onstage may present difficulties. They may feel uncomfortable with their gender identity being misread by the audience if it doesn't conform to their body. Make adjustments as desired, finding non-verbal ways to signal their unique relationship to their body. In the original production, Performer 2 didn't have a gender that corresponded to their body, so we built in certain movements to indicate that. Though it may seem contradictory to make room for markers of an individual performer's gender in an otherwise gender-fluid world, we don't wish to exclude performers for whom even the performance of fluidity feels like a denial of their existence. With that said, it shouldn't be assumed that all transgender performers will want to signal their gender identities while performing.

Each of the first nine scenes has an accompanying video projection. Unless otherwise indicated, this projection remains fixed and unchanging throughout the scene, then morphs into the projection for the next scene. There are no projections for Scenes 10 through 15. I describe the projections we used in the original production but, again, this is not meant to be prescriptive.

The original production was created for a proscenium stage, but other arrangements are certainly possible.

This document is a necessarily inadequate record of our production, because our show was built out of the particular ineffable qualities of the performers involved, and its spirit lives within them in a way that can't be scripted.

Untitled Feminist Show is meant to be a vehicle for the charismatic power of its performers. Your production can depart from the original as necessary to accommodate the talents, abilities, and identities of its performers. Nothing matters more than the performers' energy and the emotion it generates.

PART ONE

EXALTING THE DESPISED

Part One of the show is all about celebrating aspects of being human that have historically been labeled as "feminine" and therefore regarded as lesser than. We begin by welcoming these aspects into our space and acknowledging their power.

The playing space is a solid white rectangle on a black floor. Around the white rectangle there are several feet of clear space—a bit of breathing room—before any masking, walls, or equipment.

Hanging overhead is a mysterious rectangular white object, which we referred to as "the monolith." It's as long as the white rectangle of floor and bears some resemblance to the monolith in Stanley Kubrick's *2001*, except that it's white and horizontal rather than black and vertical.

A pattern of smoky, subtly shifting light is projected onto the surface of the monolith. Note: All of the images and video in the show are projected onto this surface and should be cropped to the edges so perfectly that it's hard to know if the images come from within or without.

A low rumbling plays.

1

CLEANSING RITUAL

In this scene, the performers take ownership of the entire room. By appearing where the audience doesn't expect them to appear and exchanging looks and energy with people up close, they prevent view-ers from feeling a safe, fourth-wall-protected distance from which they can evaluate the performers like objects. The performers' unison breathing, which should be vocally projected to be audible but not amplified or boosted by a recording, is meant to cleanse the room of negative energy.

Duration: Varies depending on size of the theater.

A recording of a gender-neutral voice delivers a pre-show announcement. The announcement includes a warning about strobe lights.

As the pre-show rumbling continues, Performer 1 and Per-former 2 enter from behind the audience, on opposite sides. They exhale. They walk down the aisles past the audience, stepping in unison and exhaling with each step. Dancer 2 and Dancer 3 follow a few steps behind, stepping and breathing in sync with the others.

The performers look at the audience, taking in people's reactions to their nudity. They inhale and exhale, breathing in the reactions and exhaling transformative energy, filling the room with their spirit as they move toward the stage.

The rumbling intensifies as the performers slowly and symmetrically make their way onto the stage. Dancer 1 and Performer 3 appear in the upstage corners, stepping and breathing in sync with the others until they all converge and land as follows:

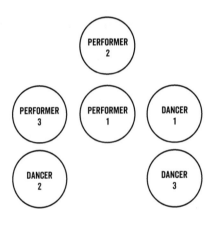

2

VENERATING THE PUSSY

In this scene, the performers exalt the pussy, as represented by the pussy of Performer 1. The scene should not be played for laughs. The audience should feel as if it is watching a sacred, ancient ritual.

Duration: Around three minutes.

On an inhale, everyone raises their arms and makes contact with each other, except Performer 1, who covers their own eyes.

We hear two slow hits of a kick drum, followed by four more in double time.

The projection changes to a fiery prismatic image that mirrors itself like a Rorschach inkblot.

A menacing drone looms over the opening beat of Lil' Kim's "Suck My Dick." A synthesizer pulses darkly alongside sirens and sprays of digital noise. Early in the dance, a steady minor bass riff emerges. As the dance builds to its climax, an organ-like synth plays insistently over the sampled sounds, gradually overtaking them until a final crash hits, coinciding with the climax of the choreography as described below. The music evokes size, strength, and power: a flag unfurling.

Moving slowly in unison, the performers create a series of symmetrical, abstract tableaux, each side a perfect reflection of the other, with Performer 1 and Performer 2 at the midline throughout. The DANCERS and Performer 3 pivot, extend their limbs, pose, and grasp each other's hair as they shift from one tableau to the next. They recall wild animals in one moment, graceful Greek sculptures in another. In the center, Performer 1 and Performer 2 coordinate their movements, making shapes, rotating, and trading places. They suggest a multiple-armed Durga goddess in one moment, Leonardo da Vinci's *Vitruvian Man* in another.

At the end of the dance, Performer 2 walks downstage and sits facing the audience, hugging their knees to cover their crotch and chest. The performers land as follows:

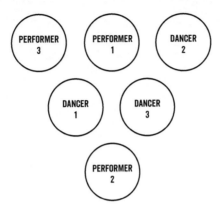

The DANCERS and Performer 3 lift Performer 1 and hold up Performer 1's legs straight in front of them. On a musical crash, they spread Performer 1's legs wide, revealing Performer 1's pussy. At the same time, Performer 2 spreads their legs wide, covering up their crotch and chest with their hands. Following the reveal and musical crash, the track becomes sparer, with some moments of industrial dissonance.

A sample of human breath creeps in, along with some synth strings as the performers move into a circle around Performer 1. The lights lower, making their bodies cast long shadows onto the floor. Everyone slowly rotates in unison and then exits, except for Performer 3, who walks to center with their back to the audience.

The lights dim.

The lights, video, and sound transition very abruptly all at once into the next scene.

3

FAIRY TALE

Up until now, the show may have been somewhat unsettling and/or "woo-woo" (that is, "hippie-ish," "new agey," etc.) for some viewers. This scene snaps the audience into a lighter mode by entertaining it with a humorous fairy tale about how, with the help of a fairy godperson, three siblings use magic parasols to defeat a witch and the witch's goblin child.

However, unlike in a traditional fairy tale, good and evil aren't clearly differentiated in this story, and the characters embody all kinds of conflicting traits. The siblings are innocent children and also cannibalistic savages. The witch is both a terrifying predator and a loving parent. In the end, the siblings are ostensibly the "winners," but our sympathy (and the sympathy of the fairy godperson) lies with the witch. It is important that the audience be able to follow the story, as in a play for children. But don't hesitate to lean into the grotesque. Although the scene is mostly comic, the ending should be disturbing and sad, and the audience's final feeling should be compassion for the witch.

Note: The names "Dorothy" and "Mary" are used not to signify gender, but as references to slang for gay men. It's a subtle joke that most people won't get, so feel free to replace the names with more gender-neutral ones if you'd prefer.

The performers play the following characters:

Performer 1	*Fairy Godperson*
Performer 2	*Middle Child*
Performer 3	*Witch*

Dancer 1	Youngest Child
Dancer 2	Oldest Child
Dancer 3	Goblin

Duration: Around ten minutes.

After all of the performers have exited except for Performer 3, abrupt lights up on the witch.

The projection switches to a forest-themed image that mirrors itself symmetrically.

We hear the sweetly trilling violin solo of Mozart's Violin Concerto No. 3 in G, K216, 1. Allegro, performed by a fifteen-year-old Anne-Sophie Mutter with the Berlin Philharmonic Orchestra. The dynamic shifts of the piece are edited to match the scene's shifts in tone.

As the lights, video, and music change, the witch spins around to face the audience, laughing maniacally. The witch concocts a magic potion, stirring earwax and vaginal discharge into a cauldron. They cast a spell over the cauldron and then take a taste. The potion enables them to transform into a frog, then a chicken, then back to their original shape. They do a celebratory jig.

The witch claps to summon their child, the goblin, who limps in. They embrace. The witch scratches behind the goblin's ear, causing the goblin's leg to shake like a happy dog's. They nuzzle each other.

The goblin indicates that they are hungry. The witch whistles to summon a bird, pets it, snaps its neck, and hands it to the goblin to eat. The goblin starts to cry and pleads with the witch to bring the bird back to life. The witch complies and hands the resurrected bird to the goblin, who nuzzles it before letting it fly away. The goblin again indicates that they are hungry.

Oldest child, middle child, and youngest child enter holding hands and skipping. The witch transforms into a tree and the goblin hides behind them.

The children play a game of London Bridge that ends in a fight between middle child and youngest child.

Youngest child pulls oldest child away to play Patty Cake, excluding and taunting middle child. Middle child forces their way into the middle of the game. This results in a shoving match between middle child and youngest child. Youngest child starts to cry ostentatiously. Oldest child forces them both into a game of Ring Around the Rosy, which gradually becomes more and more joyful.

The children hold hands and resume their skipping. The goblin comes out from behind the witch-as-tree and starts limping after the children, who run away in terror. The witch transforms back to their original shape and casts a spell that freezes the children in place. The goblin licks their lips in anticipation of eating the children.

Fairy godperson enters with four frilly pink parasols. As the witch raises their hand to cast a spell on fairy godperson, fairy godperson points a parasol at the witch and the goblin, who clutch their ears as if hearing an unbearably painful noise. Fairy godperson shakes the magic parasol at them as they stagger away in pain.

Fairy godperson waves a parasol to unfreeze the children and then hands a parasol to each of them. Fairy godperson teaches the children how to protect themselves using the parasols. After an elaborate goodbye, fairy godperson flits off in one direction while oldest child and middle child skip off in another. Youngest child lingers behind, still waving goodbye to fairy godperson. When youngest child looks for their siblings, they are gone.

The witch creeps in. Youngest child starts to play hopscotch, holding their magic parasol. The witch transforms into a very young child and toddles toward youngest child, licking an ice-cream cone. The witch offers the ice-cream cone to youngest child, demanding their parasol in exchange. Youngest child agrees to the trade, and just as youngest child sticks out their tongue to lick the cone, the witch transforms back to their original shape and freezes youngest child with a spell. The goblin drags youngest child away and starts devouring them.

Middle child enters holding their parasol and miming calling out, "Dorothy!" as they look for youngest child. The witch transforms into a stooped old woman who is having trouble walking. Middle child takes their arm and helps them along. The witch-as-old-woman pretends to stumble and fall, which causes middle child to drop their parasol. The witch transforms back to their original shape and freezes middle child with a spell. The goblin limps over and drags middle child away. The witch and the goblin celebrate.

As the goblin starts gobbling up middle child, oldest child enters holding their parasol. They mime calling out, "Mary! Mary!" The witch transforms into a handsome hunter. The witch-as-hunter and oldest child flirt shamelessly. The witch-as-hunter takes out a bow and arrow and shoots a bird out of the sky, then picks a flower and hands it to oldest child. The witch-as-hunter gets down on one knee, takes oldest child's hand, and kisses all the way up their arm. The witch-as-hunter attempts to take oldest child's parasol, but oldest child says no. The witch-as-hunter persists. They struggle over the parasol. The witch transforms back and attempts to cast a spell, but oldest child hits the witch over the head with their parasol, knocking the witch to the ground. As the goblin runs to the witch, oldest child holds their parasol in a defensive position.

The goblin checks on the unconscious witch, then furiously runs to attack oldest child, who fatally stabs the goblin in the stomach with their parasol. The goblin does a dramatic dance of death, hopping in circles and doing endless scissor kicks as oldest child looks bored. Finally, after one last spasmodic scissor kick, the goblin sprawls out on the ground, dead.

Oldest child goes to the goblin and stabs their parasol into the goblin's chest, slicing downward to open up their torso.

The music's tempo finally slows, featuring a spare violin duet.

Middle child and youngest child crawl out of the goblin's stomach as oldest child helps them up. They all wipe goblin-gore off of each other. They go to the goblin's corpse and pause for a beat before ripping savagely into the goblin's body, pulling out the goblin's entrails and gorging on them. When they are finished eating, they wipe their mouths daintily and pick their teeth before grabbing their parasols and skipping offstage, blithely hopping over the witch's unconscious body on their way out.

The witch wakes up and claps their hands repeatedly, trying to summon the goblin. They see the goblin's corpse and run to it. They frantically collect the goblin's strewn entrails and try to place them back inside their body. The witch desperately tries to cast a spell to bring the goblin back to life, but nothing works. The witch cries out in despair. They gently cross the goblin's arms over their chest and nuzzle their face.

Fairy godperson approaches the witch holding a parasol. The witch puts their hand up to cast a defensive spell, but subsides when fairy godperson kneels down next to them, putting their arm around the witch. After a long pause filled with grief, the witch places their hand on top of fairy godperson's. Fairy godperson brings their parasol down to end the scene as the music concludes traditionally with a grand tonic.

4

PARASOL DANCE

In this scene, the performers express the joy of "girly femininity," of skipping and twirling and frilly pinkness; to take what is despised in patriarchal society as weak and childish and show the power of the joy within it. This scene should not be comic, as if making fun of "femininity." Rather, the joyous athleticism of the performers should fill the audience with envious admiration.

Note: This scene isn't meant to be any kind of statement about what women are or should be. Rather, it creates space for one way of being human that has been stripped of its power by misogyny.

The same pink, frilly parasols from the last scene are also used here.

Duration: Around two minutes.

The tree in the projection from the last scene begins to rotate clockwise, turning into a refractive geometric pattern that morphs into a fluffy pink-and-white pattern that evokes cotton candy, petals, and clouds.

As Dancer 1, Dancer 2, and Performer 2 enter spinning frilly pink parasols in their hands, the cheerful piano chord pattern that opens The Magnetic Fields' "100,000 Fireflies" fades up. The chords play repetitively over a robotic drum beat.

Dancer 1, Dancer 2, and Performer 2 hand parasols to Dancer 3 and Performer 3, and everyone comes together to giggle and gossip in a cluster, with their parasols resting on their shoulders.

The PERFORMERS then run to opposite corners of the stage and pose, creating a frame for the DANCERS, who perform an exuberant, athletically challenging unison dance with complex and symmetrical floor patterns. The DANCERS flourish and twirl their parasols as they dance: leaping, spinning, kicking, and prancing in varied formations. Partway through their dance, the robotic drum pattern picks up and develops a rumbling quality, creating a feeling of speed and lightness.

The DANCERS whirl out to the corners of the stage as the PERFORMERS twirl back in. A new melody emerges as the dainty piano solo from the instrumental break of "100,000 Fireflies" plays, and the DANCERS pose to create a frame for the PERFORMERS, who do a pretty dance of their own: spinning, swooping, and thrusting their parasols. The PERFORMERS end their dance spinning, and the DANCERS emerge from their corners while spinning around each other. They all twirl toward center stage with their parasols up.

They land as follows, creating a giant flower shape with their parasols facing the audience:

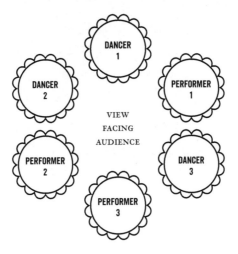

They spin their parasols at the audience, beaming with happiness.

The original cheerful piano chord repetitions return, accompanied by a sparkling chimes and a four-on-the-floor kick-drum pattern that builds to a triumphant conclusion.

The PERFORMERS twirl out to the edges of the stage and pose, while the DANCERS whirl into a triangle formation center stage and do another complicated unison dance.

Then all the performers start weaving, taking turns leaping between each other, until they land as follows, forming two columns with their parasols facing the audience:

VIEW FACING AUDIENCE

The performers remain hidden behind their parasols as a sparkling tone, the sound of a star falling, ends the song.

5

SELF-CONFIDENCE

In this scene, Dancer 2 conveys the power of self-confidence. So far, all of the performers have displayed impressive virtuosity that elevates them as "special." Now Dancer 2 does something that Dancer 2 is not good at, but maintains the same level of self-belief and joy as before. Dancer 2 is not delusional—they know they are not a strong singer—but they sing their heart out nonetheless because they love to do it, and because they know their charisma is infectious. This scene should be funny, but the audience should laugh with Dancer 2 rather than at them, and admire Dancer 2's moxie. Dancer 2 should not seem obnoxiously conceited, but fabulous with a sense of humor about themself.

There should be no music other than Dancer 2's singing.

Duration: Around three minutes.

During the star-falling music that concludes the previous scene, the cotton-candy-clouds projection dissolves into a glimmering, kaleidoscopic, ocean-toned jewel pattern that mirrors itself symmetrically. As the projection shifts, the performers swing out their parasols to reveal Dancer 2, who steps through with great aplomb and begins singing a recognizable R&B song (such as SWV's "Weak") using "la la la"s instead of words. Dancer 2 is comically off-key, but they have all the charisma and attitude of a world-class diva. The other performers sweep offstage.

After finishing the first verse, Dancer 2 pauses. We might think they're finished, but they continue on to the second verse with even more intensity, beginning some light choreography. They connect with the audience, presenting their singing as a gift. They are a star. They walk and twirl across the stage, making sure to connect with people on both sides of the audience. They sing up to the cheap seats. They single out a few audience members here and there, pointing and winking as if to say, "This one's for you." When Dancer 2 gets to the second chorus, they add a Fosse-esque kick, becoming increasingly showy.

The other performers (minus Performer 1—see note at the top of next scene) reenter from the wings, stepping and clapping to the beat of the song like backup dancers. They slide into a line behind Dancer 2, clapping and stepping from side to side as the song comes to an end. Dancer 2 holds a climactic note for an impossibly long time before finishing with a soft vocal flourish.

Dancer 2 raises one arm regally and lowers into a deep curtsy while the other performers applaud. The audience *must* applaud.

6

DOMESTIC LABOR

In this scene, the performers exalt the domestic labor historically regarded as "women's work" and therefore despised and undervalued. This highly choreographed routine turns domestic tasks into hip-hop moves. The performers do not smile at the audience. They are fiercely focused on their tasks. The dance demonstrates that domestic work is hard and serious skilled labor that should command respect and be paid accordingly. In the original production, we found that the formations worked better with five performers than with six, so Performer 1 didn't participate. This dance should make the audience feel awe and respect. The performers should not mime venerating each other's work—they should focus on doing their jobs with earned pride.

Duration: Around three minutes.

As the clapping fades from the previous scene and the lights shift, the performers rearrange into a downstage-pointing V with their backs to the audience.

As soon as they hit their marks, Dancer 1 shouts "HO!" and the performers spin to face the audience.

The stage goes dark except for five bright white boxes of light that spotlight each of the performers, and the previous jewel-kaleidoscope projection is knocked out by a colorful square-themed image that mirrors itself symmetrically.

Also on the "HO!," the flute opening of N.O.R.E.'s "Nothin'" begins to play. Over the course of the dance, sound layers come in and out of the N.O.R.E. track, corresponding to shifts in choreography. At various points we'll hear bongos, clanks, cymbal taps, percussive breathing, buzzing synths, a driving bass line, record scratching, zaps, bubbling, revving, and hand claps that enter and exit the track to differentiate choreographic sections and punctuate key moves. Looped vocal decorations—"yo!," "woo!," "uh!," etc.—also come in and out, evoking the feeling of a party dance floor.

The performers stand facing the audience, looking forward intensely as the lights brighten. After four bars, the beat drops and they raise their left arms sharply into a curved position in front of them as if holding a giant bowl. In unison, they raise their right arms as if reaching for something out of a cupboard. Performer 3, who is at the downstage point of the V, mimes taking something out of a cabinet, then shakes it into their bowl while bouncing up and down. The other performers follow in a canon (that is, with the same movement being started at different points in time successively).

The performers toss more ingredients into their bowls in rhythm with the music. They stir the contents of their bowls slowly in large round circles, circling their hips in the same direction. Performer 3 lowers themself down to the floor sexily while beating. The other performers follow suit in a canon.

They all stand up, turn to their left, and scoop their arms forward as if picking up a baby. They breastfeed, then bounce their babies. While bouncing their babies, they run with them and land as follows:

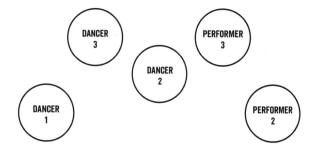

They drop to their hands and knees, mime dunking rags into buckets, and make circles on the floor with their hands in a scrubbing motion. They stand and squirt spray bottles this way and that. Making window-squeegee-ing, body-rolling motions, they land as follows:

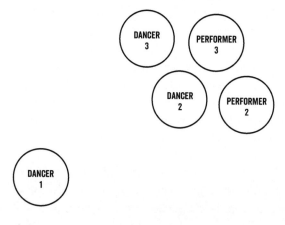

They scrub at a spot on an imaginary window, then freeze. Dancer 1 begins a solo in which they yank down a piece of laundry and expertly prep it for ironing. As Dancer 1 reaches for an iron, the other performers unfreeze and join Dancer 1 in funky ironing.

The performers switch to scolding and chasing a toddler, which travels them back to their earlier floor-scrubbing positions. Some of the performers scrub the floor while others wash dishes, then they switch.

They mop their way into a V with an upstage-facing point. They make sandwiches, then feed babies, making airplanes with their spoons to coax the babies while moving into a diagonal line. The performers bounce their babies, make faces at them, and change their diapers. They pick up the diapers and throw them away, holding their noses.

They pick up mops, spin, squeeze their mops into buckets, and freeze. They unfreeze to sweep their way into a vertical line facing the audience. In a canon, they sweep out to the sides and spring back to the vertical line.

They wheel imaginary grocery carts and land as follows:

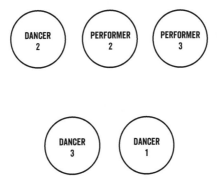

They wave as if running into each other at the grocery store, then proceed to shop. Dancers 1 and 3 cross upstage while the others cross downstage. They all land momentarily as follows:

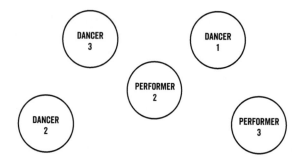

In unison, they all select a piece of fruit, smell it, and throw it away. They run into position to create a "human vacuum," as below:

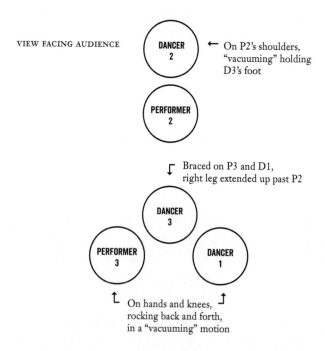

Dancer 2 vacuums. When the vacuuming is done, Dancer 1 and Performer 3 cartwheel out. Dancer 3 makes broom-pushing motions downstage. Dancer 2 holds their arm out in the original bowl position and mimes reaching for an ingredient and shaking it in. Everyone lifts their arm to make a bowl, stirs twice, and freezes as the music abruptly stops.

PART TWO

MOVING TOWARD FLUIDITY

Now that Part One of the show has uplifted and celebrated the despised "feminine," in Part Two we can move on to exploring and embracing a variety of other aspects of being human, many of which have been traditionally deemed off-limits for women. In Part Two, we also attempt to bypass the intellect's binary programming (that is, the programming that causes us to see things as being either one thing or another) and encourage the audience to embrace shape-shifting and fluidity.

7

CRUDE HUMOR

In this scene, Performer 3 makes the audience laugh with an absurdly raunchy routine.

Note: In this scene, Performer 3 picks cis men out of the audience and mimes ludicrously extreme sexual acts with them. Cis men refers here not just to actual cis men but also to people who are perceived as cis men by Performer 3.

If the performer picks someone who initially seems open to being approached, but looks truly distressed as things progress, they should mime their sincere apologies and start over with a new person.

While part of the fun of this scene is about turning the tables on cis men, the scene should be performed with playful good humor rather than vindictive malice. Performer 3 should seek out people who seem open to an interaction, and that interaction should always have gleeful stupidity at its core. The audience members selected for interaction should feel teased in a ridiculous way, not violated or shamed. The challenge is to make the potentially disturbing content feel cartoonish and funny. As in much of comedy, the idea here is to take something and exaggerate it, and then exaggerate the exaggeration. The insane sexual acts should be performed with loving, joyful exuberance. The absurd premise is that this weirdly extreme violence is fun and sexy for all involved. The most important thing is making the audience laugh.

The movement should be choreographed and specific, since the miming gets complicated and it must be clear to the audience what is happening at all times.

There should be no sound in this scene other than the audience's reactions.

Duration: Around six minutes.

The lights transition into a bright wash illuminating both stage and audience, and the color-block projection from the previous scene wobbles out of focus and bursts out of frame to reveal the next image: a hare against a bucolic landscape, mirrored symmetrically. As the lights and projection change, everyone exits except for Performer 3.

Performer 3 stands center stage, grinning and peering into the audience, looking for someone to play with. Finally, Performer 3 points at a cis male member of the audience. They flirtatiously mouth the word "hi." They wink at him and make sure he knows he's the one they're looking at. They make a quick blowjob motion, moving their hand back and forth while sticking their tongue into their cheek. They point again at the audience member and grin, indicating, "This is what I'm gonna do to you." They make the blowjob motion again, this time slowly rolling their tongue all around their mouth as if their tongue were his dick. They point at the audience member again and smile.

Abandoning their first lover, Performer 3 seeks out a new one. They point to a new cis man and wave flirtatiously. They mime jerking him off while pointing to him. They jerk him off for a while, looking at him like, "Wow, you're really loving this!" While continuing to jerk him off, Performer 3 reaches with their free hand to fondle his balls. They abandon his dick to fondle his balls with both hands, then point at him again. They goofily go back and forth between tickling one ball and then the other, alternating hands. They slap his balls a little too hard with a mischievous expression. They tug on his dick and balls, again a little too hard, grinning flirtatiously. They take out a pair of imaginary scissors and slowly cut off his balls, looking at him and nodding reassuringly as if to say, "We're doing this in the context of a loving relationship."

Once his balls have been cut off, Performer 3 suddenly stuffs them into their mouth. They passionately teabag his severed balls and then, just as quickly, return the balls to their original location and sew them lovingly back on, one tender stitch at a time. When the sewing is done, Performer 3 snaps the imaginary thread with their teeth and goes back to fondling his balls as before. They point at the audience member, wink, and give his balls one last twiddle before swaggering on to their next lover.

Performer 3 walks to the other side of the stage, peering into the cheap seats, and this time points out two cis men sitting in different parts of the theater. Very suddenly, Performer 3 mimes frantically jerking them both off at the same time, mouth open and tongue outstretched to catch every drop of their cum. Performer 3 gets cum in their eye and pauses to wipe it off, then resumes jerking the audience members off into their mouth, moving quickly back and forth between the two dicks. There's so much cum that Performer 3 rubs it into their armpits and all over their torso.

As Performer 3 slows down the pace of this double jerk-off, they start contemplating the two dicks and get a sexy idea. They gradually bring the dicks closer and closer together, becoming increasingly excited. Performer 3 eventually makes the two dicks touch, pressing their tips together while making kissing sounds.

Performer 3 starts rotating the dicks around each other and is amazed to find that they can be twisted together like carnival balloons. Performer 3 twists the dicks together higher and higher, incredulous at how far they can go, and finally ties them into a bow at the top.

Performer 3 ecstatically strokes the twisted-together dicks up and down with both hands, gives both sets of balls a quick twiddle, then goes back to stroking before suddenly grabbing an imaginary ax and chopping the conjoined dicks like a lumberjack chopping down a tree. Performer 3 points at the two audience members, beaming, and takes turns winking at first one and then the other with alternating eyes.

Performer 3 looks out into the audience and points at a new cis male. Performer 3 reaches around to mime grabbing his dick, but then changes their mind and cups his butt cheeks instead, pointing at him to indicate, "This is your butt." Performer 3 lightly slaps one of his butt cheeks, and then lowers themself until they are eye-level with his butt. Performer 3 repositions their hands to spread apart his butt cheeks and kneels on the floor, looking at the audience member inquiringly, as if asking for his consent. Performer 3 brings their tongue gradually closer to his asshole and begins licking it up and down. They look at him, mouthing the words "so good." Performer 3 licks their forefinger all over and inserts it into the audience member's asshole. Looking at him inquiringly all the while, they start jabbing their finger in and out. Excited by this, Performer 3 licks their entire hand and starts gingerly trying to insert their entire hand up his asshole, still looking at him inquiringly. They work at the entrance for a bit, lick their hand some more to provide additional lubrication, and gradually twist their entire hand all the way up his asshole.

To Performer 3's surprise, their hand keeps going all the way up through the audience member's body. Performer 3 frantically mouths, "I can't stop," as they twist their arm up further and further until it finally emerges from his mouth, at which point Performer 3 moves their hand like a flapping mouth and makes panicked noises, using the audience member as a human hand puppet. Then, as if the hand puppet had said, "You've gone too far!" Performer 3 rapidly works their arm back down with an apologetic expression until their hand finally pops back out. Performer 3 sniffs their finger appreciatively and points it at the audience member. Winking, Performer 3 voraciously smells their entire arm and gestures again at the audience member, giving him full credit for everything. With the same hand, Performer 3 makes a "call me" gesture.

8

TENDERNESS

In this scene, Performer 3 transitions effortlessly from crude, violent humor to loving, vulnerable tenderness. The moment that Performer 3 starts to sing, the audience should forget the preceding scene and be caught up in the emotion of the song. This is an important first step in the audience's journey through fluidity of identity. The audience can't reduce Performer 3 to the raunchiness just displayed, but must recognize Performer 3 as a multifaceted human being.

I chose the Welsh song "Ar Lan y Môr" because it's beautiful and because the likelihood of anyone in the audience being able to understand the lyrics seems low. (If performing the song in Wales, you should pick another song.) This scene should make the audience go completely silent and still.

There should be no sound in this scene other than the performer's singing.

Duration: Around two minutes.

Performer 3 looks out at the audience, dispelling the mood of the previous scene with a grave, tender energy.

The projection transitions from the doubled hare to a delicate lithograph of trees. Tree branches fan out against a faint mountainous background. The image mirrors itself symmetrically.

PERFORMER 3 *(Singing)*:
    Ar lan y môr mae rhosys cochion
    Ar lan y môr mae lilis gwynion
    Ar lan y môr mae 'nghariad inne
    Yn cysgu'r nos a chodi'r bore.

    Ar lan y môr mae carreg wastad
    Lle bûm yn siarad gair â'm cariad
    O amgylch hon fe dyf y lili
    Ac ambell gangen o rosmari.

    Ar lan y môr mae cerrig gleision
    Ar lan y môr mae blodau'r meibion
    Ar lan y môr mae pob rinweddau
    Ar lan y môr mae nghariad innau.

Performer 3 exits.

9

LESBIAN LOVE

Due to the erasure of that which is perceived as feminine within patriarchal societies, lesbians have received too little recognition or representation, and the purpose of this scene is to celebrate their love. To that end, Dancer 2 and Dancer 3—whether AFAB or AMAB— should both identify as women.

Dancer 3 must be able to lift Dancer 2. If Dancer 2 can also lift Dancer 3, then all the better. The choreography shouldn't allow the audience to identify either performer as the "top" or the "bottom" in the relationship. Each should get to pursue and be pursued.

This dance is a celebration of falling in love when a relationship is new. The yearning, romance, desire, and eventual love between the partners should feel very real and moving to the audience.

Duration: Around four minutes.

The plucked bass guitar melody from the opening of Grizzly Bear's cover of The Crystals' "He Hit Me (And It Felt Like A Kiss)" begins to play. Over the course of the dance, new sound elements enter and exit the track, corresponding to stages in the lovers' romance: a misty, shimmering sound-scape made of blurry bells and an organ; dreamy synth strings; angelic pirouetting "ooohs"; the crashing cymbals and soaring guitars of the Grizzly Bear track's instrumental break.

As the music starts, the lights shift romantically and the delicate-trees projection is gradually overtaken by red, orange, and fuchsia tones that resolve into a dreamy pattern of abstract, out-of-focus blobs. Over the course of the scene, the color blobs shift subtly, intensifying and fading, rising to the fore-ground and retreating back again.

Dancer 2 and Dancer 3 enter and perform a romantic, lyrical dance in which they switch back and forth between tradition-ally "masculine" and "feminine" roles. The emotion they feel is so passionate, it can only be expressed in kicks, leaps, splits, lifts, spins, and (if possible) flips.

The narrative below shouldn't be interpreted too literally. The scene should be a flowing dance, not a sequence of theatrically mimed events.

The lovers begin as strangers and have a tentative and gradual period of courtship.

They gradually establish trust and share a moment of tenderness, after which they enter a period of bounding, twirling euphoria that culminates in a spinning lift.

The lovers then transition to an intimate floor routine involving different cuddling positions, after which they go wild with joy in a running, leaping, whirling climax that features a *Dirty Dancing*–style lift.

Eventually, they find themselves standing facing each other on opposite corners of the stage. The lovers slowly make their way back to each other and take each other's hands as the music stops.

10

ABANDON

In this scene, the performers embody the power of sexual abandon in a space that allows and supports it.

Since the third scene, we've stayed on relatively conventional footing and the audience has been able to follow everything. Now that we've assured them we're not out to completely alienate them, we can start exploring more abstract forms of expression as we move into more intense aspects of being human.

In this dance, the performers combine their bodies to form a series of six different shapes chosen by the production. Each shape lands at a different place on the stage, so the performers must travel while transitioning from one shape to another. They must stay physically connected to each other at all times, except when traveling. Throughout the entire scene—whether holding a shape or traveling—they move up and down rapidly in a motion that is part-bounce, part-shake.

The scene is not meant to have an arc. It is meant to mesmerize with repetition. The performers bounce-shake into position, and then hit the next position with intensified bounce-shaking, again and again. Audience members should feel an instinctive desire to bounce and shake in their seats along with the performers in this scene.

Note: Scenes 10 through 15 should seamlessly melt into one another, forming one long movement. To that end, there are no projections to differentiate these scenes from each other.

Duration: Around three minutes.

Still holding Dancer 2's hand, Dancer 3 starts to laugh. Dancer 3 laughs harder and harder until their whole body starts to shake. Dancer 2 holds space for Dancer 3's laughter and starts to laugh as well. The other performers enter and gather supportively around Dancer 2 and Dancer 3, making physical contact with them and laughing as Dancer 3 continues to laugh and shake.

The instrumental opening to The Knife's "We Share Our Mothers' Health" starts to play. All of the performers begin to shake subtly and connect to each other physically as they make their way into their first shape. As soon as they hit their position, the beat drops and they start full-on bounce-shaking. They all have the facial expressions of people having the greatest, craziest sex of their lives. These are not porn-faces meant to gratify the male gaze, but rather the perfectly un-self-conscious sex-faces of people who have given themselves over completely to pleasure and don't care at all what they look like. They maintain their sex-faces—which go through a variety of changes—throughout the entire scene, along with the bounce-shaking.

The performers bounce-shake their way to their second shape. When they hit their position, the intro's second beat-drop occurs and the bounce-shaking intensifies.

The performers bounce-shake their way to their third shape. When they hit their position, an ominous bass line enters and the bounce-shaking intensifies.

The performers bounce-shake their way to their fourth shape as the bass line continues.

The performers bounce-shake their way to their fifth shape. When they hit their position, the song's instrumental break plays and the bounce-shaking intensifies.

The performers bounce-shake their way to their sixth shape. When they hit their position, the drums drop out as they all continue to bounce-shake except for Dancer 1, who stands in the center and slowly lifts their head to look at the audience.

11

AGGRESSION

In this scene, Dancer 1 embodies and embraces the power of aggression and rage in a way that is pure heavy metal.

The scene should be tremendously exciting, and is not intended to be comic. The audience will ideally start screaming as if Dancer 1 were a rock star.

Duration: Around three minutes.

Still looking at the audience, Dancer 1 starts bounce-shaking more violently. The other performers take notice and sit back, holding space for Dancer 1. Dancer 1 starts shaking and punching their fists as the other performers look on supportively.

The dissonant metal guitar solo from the instrumental opening of Death's "Flesh and the Power It Holds" begins to play. Dancer 1 starts to bounce-shake aggressively, thrashing their long hair and punching their fists. Dancer 1 bounce-thrashes up to Performer 2, bracing against them while pushing them backward. Performer 2 permits this for a while, then gently pushes Dancer 1 in a different direction. Dancer 1 briefly goes to Performer 1 and then Dancer 2, bracing against each of them and bounce-thrashing. Shaking and headbanging violently, Dancer 1 braces against Dancer 3, who holds on to Dancer 1 with full strength and support. Dancer 1 pushes away from Dancer 3, and the other performers move to the sides of the stage where they stand and watch supportively, holding space for Dancer 1's rage.

As the metal beat drops, Dancer 1 makes their way to the center of the stage and performs a powerful, rage-filled abstract dance solo involving a lot of headbanging. Dancer 1's long hair flies around, part of the choreography. As the music track shifts to the instrumental break at 1:20 of Death's "Misanthrope," Dancer 1 thrashes their way to the front of the white rectangular playing area and jumps over the footlights into the audience.

Dancer 1 headbangs into the faces of everyone in the front row. As the music track shifts to the instrumental opening of Cannibal Corpse's "Decency Defied" (two seconds in), Dancer 1 thrashes their way up a theater aisle and braces themself on an audience member, headbanging wildly in the person's face. Still headbanging, Dancer 1 makes the devil-horns symbol with one hand, inviting the audience to cheer.

As the music track shifts to the instrumental opening of Morbid Angel's "Immortal Rites" (ten seconds in), Dancer 1 thrashes back down the stairs and charges directly at Performer 2, who catches Dancer 1 and pushes them away. Dancer 1 charges at Dancer 3, who catches Dancer 1 and pushes them away.

12

VIOLENCE

In this scene, Performer 1 and Dancer 1 embody and acknowledge the human quality of violence. The scene starts as a moment of comedy: a cartoonish slow-motion fight set to dreamy music. But the fight is a fight to the death, and should be brutal and gruesome enough to leave the audience disturbed by what happens in the end.

After the song starts, everything is in slow motion.

Duration: Around four minutes.

When Dancer 3 catches Dancer 1 and pushes them away, the music cuts out and Performer 1 charges toward Dancer 1, screaming with rage. Performer 1 raises a fist to punch Dancer 1 in the face. A dreamy-sounding repeating bass note starts to play, and the action switches to slow motion for the rest of the scene.

The track that accompanies this scene is made up primarily of different parts of Spiritualized's version of the song "Any Way That You Want Me" with the vocals blurred out. Comforting and hypnotic, the music soothes, evoking sensations of rotating, floating, and drifting toward a sunset. Additional sonic elements come in and out.

In slow motion, Performer 1 tries to punch Dancer 1 in the face, but Dancer 1 blocks the punch.

The other performers react in slow motion on the sidelines, some cheering (Performer 2 is particularly thirsty for blood), others wanting the violence to end. They move into a circle around the fighting pair, where they react dramatically throughout the scene.

Performer 1 and Dancer 1 engage in a slow-motion fight to the death which includes, but is not limited to: biting, tripping, hair-pulling, face-punching, breast- and face-elbowing, nose-breaking (with palm), punching and kicking of the vagina, repeated-head-slamming-into-the-ground, and choking.

The fight ends with both fighters on the ground, Performer 1 face-down and Dancer 1 face-up.

Performer 1 starts to lift their head. With a sudden final burst of energy, Dancer 1 rolls over and slams Performer 1's head into the ground—a death blow. Dancer 1 collapses back onto the floor.

Performer 2, miming a victory scream, lifts Dancer 1's limp arm and high-fives it.

13

SEDUCTIVENESS

In this scene, Performer 1 embodies the power of sensuality and seductiveness via a super-sexy traditional burlesque dance.

Performer 1 transitions effortlessly from violence to sexiness here. This is very much a performance for the audience, and Performer 1 is in total control.

This is the only moment in the show where the audience is invited to get turned on by a performer's body. Ideally, everyone will get turned on regardless of their sexual orientation.

Duration: Around one minute.

As Performer 2 drops Dancer 1's arm and walks away, the ominous electric bass riff from the instrumental intro to Radiohead's "The National Anthem" fades in. On the cymbal crash, Performer 1's head lifts.

Over the course of the track, a fuzzy distorted guitar gets layered in and goes through all sorts of noisy, droning variations.

A layer of agitated arrhythmic percussion comes through. The track is a winding snake.

Performer 1 pushes seductively up to their hands and knees, dangling their breasts. They sit up onto their heels, running their hands sensually up their body, pushing their breasts together, running their fingers through their hair.

Slowly they stand, tracing their hands up one extended leg as if putting on a stocking. They run their hands up to their breasts, squeezing them and pushing them together. Moving their hips in small circles, they strike a pinup pose, one hand on their hip, the other running through their hair.

They perform a traditional hip-swinging burlesque dance sequence, alternately covering and revealing body parts. They repeat it three times.

On the third repetition, Performer 2, who has been standing behind Performer 1, moves forward copying Performer 1's movements. Standing back-to-back, Performer 1 and Performer 2 repeat the sequence a fourth time. They rotate to switch positions and Performer 1 exits.

14

FLUIDITY

In this scene, Performer 2 deepens the audience's sense of fluidity by embodying a series of contrasting identities. If Performer 2 is uncomfortable performing any of the identities indicated below, by all means change them. But the identities should include a mix of roles considered "masculine" and "feminine" in dominant Western thought. The scene showcases Performer 2's acting ability as they embody wildly different characters in rapid succession. The audience should feel that they are watching a virtuoso performance, and they should laugh until the point indicated at the end.

Duration: Around four minutes.

As the music from the burlesque sequence fades out, Performer 2 starts singing a showbiz-sounding tune under their breath using the sounds "dah-dah-dadah."

There is no sound in this scene other than Performer 2's singing.

Still singing "dah-dah-dadah," Performer 2 crosses the stage self-consciously, doing a grapevine step and making tentative jazz hands. At the end of the line they add a little showbiz kick. Repeating this movement in the other direction, they grow more confident, singing out and transforming into a seasoned old-time Broadway entertainer.

They give the audience a mischievous chest-shimmy, then transform into a boxer, punctuating the "dah-dah-dadah"s with grunts.

The boxer morphs into an old person with a cane, hobbling across the stage and singing in an asthmatic voice.

The old person transforms into an extremely drunk asshole who sings defiantly at the audience while staggering across the stage.

The drunk asshole turns into a person having a hysterical hissy fit, screaming out the song tearfully and vomiting from the force of their own distress.

The hysterical person suddenly turns into a suave, swaggering, macho person who sings to the audience as if hitting on them.

The macho person starts sashaying and singing sassily, snapping the fingers of one hand.

The sassy person transforms into an ashamed person, covering up their chest and crotch and looking at the audience with a pained expression, singing uncomfortably under their breath. (This is the first moment where any performer shows any sign of shame, and it should not be funny.)

The ashamed person transforms back into the original Broadway jazz-hands person, but this time their towering confidence comes across as almost demonic. They make a gigantic, dramatic, virtuoso finish.

They drop their arms and stand panting, looking out at the audience as the audience applauds.

15

FLUIDITY FINALE

This scene builds to full-fledged fluidity, in which the performers transform from one identity to another with effortless joy at dizzying speed. The audience should feel overwhelmed by the performers' freedom and power to fully express all aspects of themselves without judgment.

This scene is a collage of flashbacks to previous scenes mixed with new material that pushes everything to a more intense level and creates a feeling of euphoria.

Whenever the performers travel, they embody a different identity—one from earlier in the show or an entirely new one. Sometimes two or more of them share a single identity and move in unison.

Whenever formations occur, they should seem to appear out of nowhere. The audience should be so preoccupied watching the interesting ways that performers travel to their positions that each new formation takes them by surprise.

Like Scene 10, this scene is not meant to have an arc, but unlike Scene 10, it should not feel repetitive. If Scene 10 is fluidity of identity for beginners, then this is the advanced course, with new shapes and identities flowering and exploding out from every corner.

Duration: Around five minutes.

The opening of Fischerspooner's "Emerge" begins to play. The track for this scene is made up of different instrumental parts from "Emerge," with many additional sonic elements layered in. The music and drum patterns shift frequently, but the sustained tempo of the track's futuristic beat keeps the music droning and hypnotic. Each new layer and shift in the music bring a feeling of flight and exploration, of going deeper into a world, a journey unfolding.

As the music begins, the other performers enter one by one to join Performer 2. They land as follows:

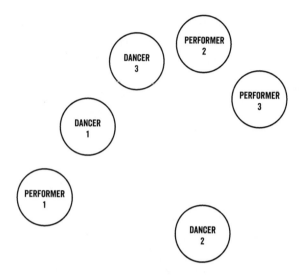

Performer 2 starts to shake as if possessed by a powerful energy. Performer 2 passes the energy to Dancer 3, who starts shaking as Performer 2 stops. Everyone watches Dancer 3.

Dancer 3's shaking becomes a powerful, graceful solo dance that culminates in the hunting of a wild beast. As the beat drops, Dancer 3 stabs down into the beast with an imaginary knife.

Dancer 3 rises, striking classical Grecian poses, then body-building poses. The other performers travel and land as follows:

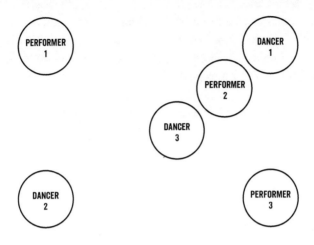

The DANCERS perform a unison dance while Performers 1 and 3 shimmy. Performer 2 hobbles downstage like an elderly person with a cane. The dance routine ends and everyone watches Dancer 2 dance a solo that resolves into a tough bouncer pose.

The bouncer pose transitions into a sexy cat-clawing motion, which transitions into a diva walk. Meanwhile, everyone travels and lands as follows:

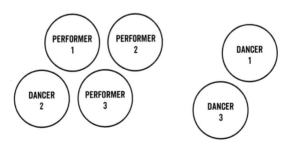

Dancers 1 and 3 entwine while striking classical Grecian poses, with the performers looking on. This transitions into a savage slow-motion fight between Dancers 1 and 3 that culminates with them biting into each other.

On the bite, everyone travels and lands as follows:

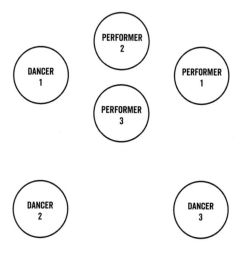

As Dancers 2 and 3 do a unison floor routine, the other performers mime looking in a mirror and sucking in their cheeks and bodies to look thinner, which turns into a goofy "Dad dance," which turns into gossiping.

Everyone travels and lands as follows:

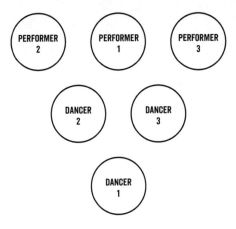

In unison, the performers each rotate clockwise in four steps. As soaring, airy strings (which will recur through the rest of the song) enter the track, the performers do the burlesque routine from Scene 13 in unison while moving downstage in formation.

They briefly revisit the fairy tale from Scene 3, traveling as their fairy tale characters to a tableau in which the witch is casting a spell, the three children are frozen, the goblin is greedily anticipating eating the children, and the fairy god-person is coming to the rescue, parasol outstretched.

The fairy tale tableau melts into a violent brawl. Dancer 1 and Performer 2 hold each other by one hand and swing in a circle while the other performers prance like show-ponies across the stage. Dancer 1 hurls Performer 2 to the floor. Performer 3 runs to the aid of Performer 2.

Everyone travels and lands as follows:

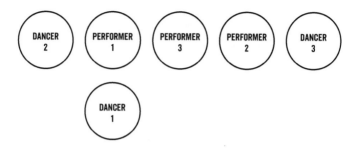

Everyone stands with their backs turned to the audience while jiggling their booties, except for Performer 2, who stands face-out covering their crotch with their hands, and Dancer 1, who looks searchingly into the audience. Dancer 1 transforms into a chatty person who can't stop babbling, then a severely depressed person.

They all travel to a new formation in which the PERFORM-ERS squat and mime pooping in the center of the stage. Dancers 2 and 3 leap and pirouette in circles around them. Dancer 1 does a solo dance in the background.

The performers all travel and land as follows:

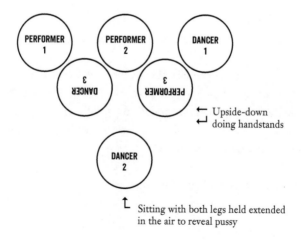

Dancer 3 and Performer 3 kick up into handstands. Their feet are caught and spread apart by Performer 1, Performer 2, and Dancer 1, who spread their own arms and legs out in an X-shape. Dancer 2, who sits on the floor in front of them, lifts Dancer 2's legs high into the air and spreads them in a V-shape.

The performers all travel and land as follows:

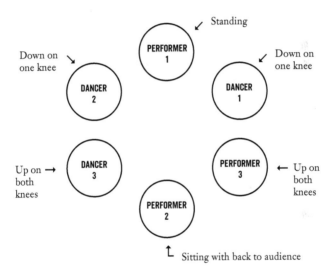

The group closes inward and then unfurls. The effect is that of a giant, fluttering flower. The flower closes again and slowly transforms into a wave of monstrous creatures, coming toward the audience in slow motion with their claws out and their mouths agape in silent, horrifying screams. Performer 1 leads the pack, screaming and advancing powerfully in slow motion while the others follow, their bodies moving up and down like crashing waves made of monsters.

The performers all exit except for Dancers 1 and 3.

Dancer 1 is kneeling on all fours in the center of the stage with their hair hanging over their face. Dancer 3 stands behind them. As the music fades, Dancer 3 reaches forward and carefully grasps Dancer 1's hair with both hands, pulling it back to reveal Dancer 1's euphoric face.

16

FLUIDITY VIDEO

This scene basically does everything that the previous scene just did, but with abstract visual imagery. We see familiar projections from earlier in the show, mixed with new images we haven't seen yet. The video should build tension throughout and explode at the end. The audience should feel overpowered by so much visual and aural intensity. The audience should feel overwhelmed by a multiplicity of possibilities so vast that the mind cannot contain them all.

Note: The intense strobe effect in this video could cause seizures.

The practical function of this scene is to give the performers time to get dressed before the curtain call.

Duration: Around three minutes.

Lights go to blackout and we hear an ambient crashing noise followed by the bassy sound of a digital void, with looping swirls and static. The sound evokes a broken satellite in space, falling down, down, down.

The white monolith hanging over the space begins to glow and slowly descend. After descending, it glows brighter and brighter to the sound of a digital whoosh. There is a split-second blackout in silence, and then an explosion of sound and image.

The panning tremolo effect from the opening of Atlas Sound's "Ready, Set, Glow" begins. Throughout this track, bits of music from earlier songs come in and out. There are no drums, but the tremolo creates the feeling of a pulse. The combined effect is disorienting, overwhelming, trance-inducing.

The monolith is inundated with ever-shifting images that morph and melt into each other in a strobing, kaleidoscopic frenzy. The effect is mesmerizing. Images we saw projected earlier come in and out, in sync with traces of the music that previously accompanied them. As the music builds, the images flash faster and faster until, with a deafening sound of explosive digital bursts, the video appears to implode, leaving the monolith white as before.

In the darkness, we listen again to the falling-satellite sound that was playing before the video started.

17

CURTAIN CALL

The purpose of this scene is to introduce the audience to the performers as the people they are in real life, to give the performers an opportunity to signal their gender identities if they wish, and to acknowledge the performers by name. It's also meant to bring the audience out of our fantasy world and back into the real world in a way that's fun and playful rather than jarring.

Duration: Around three minutes.

With a digital whoosh, lights come up on the PERFORM-ERS, standing far upstage in a row, fully dressed in their own clothes.

The floor and monolith are glowing bright white.

When the audience starts to applaud, electronic dance music kicks in and the performers walk in a line toward the audience. The beat drops when they reach the front, and they swerve upstage, forming two parallel vertical lines with a "runway" in the center.

Each performer dances down the "runway" in their own style. As they do so, their name is projected in big letters on the monolith. At the end of the runway, each performer does a special move.

After everyone has taken a turn, they come together in a line downstage for their final bows.

END

STRAIGHT
WHITE
MEN

FOR AARON ROSENBLUM

This version of *Straight White Men* opened at Second Stage Theater (Carole Rothman, President and Artistic Director) in New York City on July 23, 2018. It was directed by Anna D. Shapiro. The dramaturg was Mike Farry. The scenic design was by Todd Rosenthal. The costume design was by Suttirat Larlarb. The sound design was by M. L. Dogg. The lighting design was by Donald Holder. The choreography was by Faye Driscoll. The production stage manager was Jane Grey. The stage manager was Brian Bogin. It was performed by:

Kate Bornstein	PERSON IN CHARGE 1
Ty Defoe	PERSON IN CHARGE 2
Stephen Payne	ED
Paul Schneider	MATT
Josh Charles	JAKE
Armie Hammer	DREW

Earlier versions of *Straight White Men* were produced in the following productions:

Straight White Men opened at Steppenwolf Theatre (Anna D. Shapiro, Artistic Director; David Schmitz, Executive Director) in Chicago on February 2, 2017. It was directed by Young

Jean Lee. The dramaturg was Mike Farry. The associate director was Jessica L. Fisch. The scenic design was by David Evans Morris. The costume design was by Enver Chakartash. The original music and remixes were by Chris Giarmo. The sound design was by Jamie McElhinney. The lighting design was by Sarah Hughey. The choreography was by Faye Driscoll. The stage manager was Laura D. Glenn. It was performed by:

Elliott Jenetopulos	PERSON IN CHARGE 1
Will Wilhelm	PERSON IN CHARGE 2
Alan Wilder	ED
Brian Slaten	MATT
Madison Dirks	JAKE
Ryan Hallahan	DREW

Straight White Men opened at The Public Theater (Oskar Eustis, Artistic Director; Patrick Willingham, Executive Director) in New York City on November 17, 2014. It was directed by Young Jean Lee. It was produced by Aaron Rosenblum. The dramaturg was Mike Farry. The associate director was Emilyn Kowaleski. The scenic design was by David Evans Morris. The costume design was by Enver Chakartash. The original music and remixes were by Chris Giarmo. The sound design was by Jamie McElhinney. The lighting design was by Christopher Kuhl. The choreography was by Faye Driscoll. The production stage manager was Stephanie Byrnes Harrell. It was performed by:

Elliott Jenetopulos	STAGEHAND-IN-CHARGE
Austin Pendleton	ED
James Stanley	MATT
Gary Wilmes	JAKE
Pete Simpson	DREW

Straight White Men opened at the Wexner Center for the Arts (Charles Helm, Director of Performing Arts) in Columbus, Ohio, on April 10, 2014, with the same creative team as The Public Theater production. It was performed by:

Austin Pendleton	ED
James Stanley	MATT
Scott Shepherd	JAKE
Pete Simpson	DREW

Special thanks to Michael Chiboucas, Will Peterson, Zachary Segel, Gerrit Thurston, and all of the other students at Brown University who were part of this show's initial development, and to Frank Boyd, Corey Brill, Patch Darragh, and Richard Riehle, who performed in tours of the show.

Straight White Men was co-commissioned by The Public Theater, the Wexner Center for the Arts at The Ohio State University, Center Theatre Group, steirischer herbst festival, Festival d'Automne à Paris, and Les spectacles vivants du Centre Pompidou. It was produced by Young Jean Lee's Theater Company (Young Jean Lee, Artistic Director; Aaron Rosenblum, Producing Director).

Funding support for *Straight White Men* was generously provided by the Doris Duke Performing Artist Awards program; the New England Foundation for the Arts' National Theater Project, with lead funding from The Andrew W. Mellon Foundation; the MAP Fund, supported by the Doris Duke Charitable Foundation and The Andrew W. Mellon Foundation; the National Endowment for the Arts; and the New York State Council on the Arts, a state agency.

Straight White Men was developed at Brown University's Department of Theatre Arts and Performance Studies in Providence, Rhode Island. Residency support was provided by the Park Avenue Armory, SPACE on Ryder Farm, Spaceworks NYC, and Columbia University.

Straight White Men received its British premiere at Southwark Playhouse, London, on November 10, 2021. It was produced by David Adkin and Panorama Productions. It was directed by Steven Kunis. The movement direction was by Christina Fulcher. The set design was by Suzu Sakai. The costume design was by Beth Colley. The lighting design was by Rajiv Pattani. The sound design was by Mwen. The casting was by Lucy Casson. The production coordinator was Adam Line. The production manager was James Anderton. The company stage manager was Chloe Wilson. The assistant stage manager was Victoria Rose. It was performed by:

Kim Tatum	PERSON IN CHARGE 1
Kamari Roméo	PERSON IN CHARGE 2
Simon Rouse	ED
Charlie Condou	MATT
Alex Mugnaioni	JAKE
Cary Crankson	DREW

CHARACTERS

PERSON IN CHARGE 1
PERSON IN CHARGE 2
ED, the father
MATT, the eldest
JAKE, the middle
DREW, the youngest

SETTING

Act One: a family room, Christmas Eve
Act Two: the same, Christmas Day
Act Three: the same, the next day

NOTES

The pre-show music, curtain speech, and transitions are an important part of this play. They should create a sense that the show is under the control of people who are not straight white men. Despite this framing, the play should be performed sincerely and without irony, since it doesn't work if it is presented as a parody of straight white male behavior.

Choreography is also essential to this play. There are many moments of physical comedy in this show that are not strictly naturalistic and must be painstakingly choreographed and drilled to create maximum impact. I would strongly recommend working with a choreographer on every physical moment in the show.

Ideally, Person in Charge 1 and Person in Charge 2 should be played by transgender or nonbinary performers (preferably of color). A good-faith effort should be made to find such performers, but I'm open to variants depending on circumstances. If you wish to cast a particular cisgender performer who represents an especially marginalized group in your community (for example, Torres Strait Islander people in Australia), I am open to that. In no case should actors be cast to perform identities other than their own. Also essential: an abundance of natural charm.

Because the opening speech should be in the voices of the People in Charge and express their points of view, the performers should be very clear on why they want to participate in the production and be prepared to collaborate on their own text.

From the moment the house opens, Person in Charge 1 and Person in Charge 2 will be interacting with the audience, and they should be empowered to say whatever they want. They should also feel free to ad-lib responses to audience members as necessary during the curtain speech.

If possible, the stagehands should be female.

ACT ONE

Loud hip-hop with sexually explicit lyrics by female rappers plays during the pre-show. It's loud enough that people have to shout over it to be heard. The rumble of the bass makes the audience's seats vibrate.

The set is hidden behind a silver curtain with colored lights dancing on it in time with the music.

As the audience enters, Person in Charge 1 and Person in Charge 2 patrol the theater. They wear distinctive and personalized costumes that make them easily distinguishable from the ushers and audience members. It is important that the performers playing the People in Charge like their costumes and feel comfortable wearing them.

The People in Charge interact with audience members, greeting and welcoming them into the theater. If audience members seem unhappy about the pre-show music or complain, the People in Charge should listen and respond with empathy. They should never apologize for the music or say that it's not in their power to turn it down. (Please make sure they do have the authority to have it turned down in case of emergencies.) Here are some suggestions for responses:

- *Is the music too loud for you? Yeah, it's too loud for a lot of people.*
- *I have earplugs if you want earplugs.*
- *We can't turn the music down because it's part of the play, but it will all be explained to you soon.*
- *This part of the show will be over in X minutes.*
- *If you'd rather, I can take you out to the lobby, and we'll be sure to bring you back in before the play starts*

If audience members complain about the music to ushers, the ushers should reply, "I'll go get you a Person in Charge," and then alert the nearest Person in Charge. Ushers should be informed that it is okay for them to interrupt the People in Charge when they are talking to other people, so that the People in Charge know that people are waiting for them. If an audience member asks a Person in Charge for a manager, the Person in Charge should reply, "I am the Person in Charge."

At the end of the pre-show, the People in Charge walk onto the stage. Person in Charge 1 makes a gesture that cuts off the music.

The below curtain speech was written to reflect the thoughts and feelings of the performers playing the People in Charge in the 2018 Second Stage production. This speech is not meant to instruct the audience on how to interpret the play and it does not express any intent on the part of the author. Future productions should keep as much of the curtain-speech wording as possible, but change anything that doesn't reflect the identities and views of the performers speaking the lines. The curtain speech should be an opportunity for the performers playing the People in Charge to express how they actually feel about the show and to communicate what they want to say to the audience.

PERSON IN CHARGE 1: Good evening ladies, gentlemen, and the rest of us. Welcome to Second Stage Theater. I'm Kate Bornstein.

PERSON IN CHARGE 2: And I'm Ty Defoe.

PERSON IN CHARGE 1: And in case you were wondering, neither of us is a straight white man.

PERSON IN CHARGE 2: I'm from the Oneida and the Ojibwe Nations. My gender identity is niizhi manitouwug, which means "transcending gender" in the Ojibwe language.

PERSON IN CHARGE 1: Me, I'm a Jew from the Jersey Shore. And I'm what's called "nonbinary," which means "not man/not woman" in the English language.

PERSON IN CHARGE 2: Before we begin the show, we'd like to acknowledge that our pre-show music may have made some of you uncomfortable.

PERSON IN CHARGE 1: And normally when you pay money— especially Broadway money—you can expect to feel comfortable.

PERSON IN CHARGE 2: Kate and I are well aware that it can be upsetting when people create an environment that doesn't take your needs into account.

PERSON IN CHARGE 1: As for those of you who liked the music or at least you didn't mind it, please know that we deliberately set up our pre-show to cater to your experience. We wanted to make sure you'd feel welcome in this theater.

PERSON IN CHARGE 2: Congratulations on your moment of privilege.

PERSON IN CHARGE 1: And now for something we all have in common.

PERSON IN CHARGE 2: This theater we're all sitting in together is built on the land of my people. So, welcome!

When I told my friends I was doing a play called *Straight White Men*, they were like, "Uh, have they seen you?"

PERSON IN CHARGE 1: When I got invited to audition for *Straight White Men*, I thought, "Well, I've been misgendered before, but this seems extreme."

PERSON IN CHARGE 2: Living in a Western culture, I'm supposed to wanna be a straight white man. But among my people, my gender identity—niizhi manitouwug—makes me a rock star in my community. On the other hand, chimookoman—white man—not so much.

PERSON IN CHARGE 1: Me, I used to be a straight white man. Well, I tried.

Everything I really wanted to be in life could get me arrested or sent straight to hell. Trans, gay, not-man/not-woman—all of that! But now that I'm an old fart, I don't give a damn. I'm gonna be anything I wanna be. There's only one rule I care about: Don't be mean.

Listen, my darlings, it's hard enough not being mean to people you love. It's much harder not being mean to people you think you've got a good reason to hate.

PERSON IN CHARGE 2: So tonight Kate and I are here to try something a little tricky. As foreign as they are to us, we're gonna try to find some understanding for straight white men. That's what we wish everyone would do for us.

PERSON IN CHARGE 1: Now, from here on out, everything will proceed as one might expect, more or less. All of the characters will be straight white men.

PERSON IN CHARGE 2: Each of the actors will play only one character. They will stay in character and pretend not to see you, unless they hear your cell phone ring or see you taking photos or videos, in which case they may come into the audience and attack you.

PERSON IN CHARGE 1: All righty then.

(To Person in Charge 2) You ready, pal?

(Person in Charge 2 snaps their fingers to make the curtain rise.

A cheerful, guitar-based instrumental track begins while Person in Charge 1 and Person in Charge 2 exit.

The curtain rises to reveal a hypernaturalistic middle-class family room.

The room has wall-to-wall beige carpeting, taupe walls, and minimalist molding. Stage left, a linoleum-floored mudroom leads to a door to the garage. There is a storage bench next to the door with coats hanging on pegs above. In front of the bench sits an ancient exercise bike. On the other side of the door is a closet containing a washer and dryer. Around the corner is a coat closet with a dart board on it.

Center stage is a taupe leather sofa, a matching easy chair, a dark brown leather recliner with matching ottoman, a side table, and a large, battered, wooden coffee table. The focal point of the room is an unseen television downstage center. Because of this, the wall behind the sofa is oddly bare—this is the wall that no one ever looks at when they're in the room. Against this wall are two matching bookcases packed full of old books, games, puzzles, and a component stereo system. Next to the shelves sit stackable clear plastic storage bins filled with Christmas decorations and wrapping supplies.

Stage right is an unused fireplace flanked by two windows. On the fireplace mantel are Christmas cards and a hand-crocheted, multiethnic Christmas nativity scene. Stockings hang above the fireplace.

Upstage left, three carpeted steps lead up and out through a doorway leading into a hallway. The hallway runs between an unseen kitchen and living room. A door to a half-bath is visible through the doorway.

Person in Charge 2 enters leading in Drew. They guide him into position and pose him like an action figure. Drew is around forty and wears a red-plaid hunting shirt, dark skinny jeans, and patterned socks.

Overlapping with them, Person in Charge 1 leads in Jake and seats him on the sofa. Person in Charge 1 hands Jake a video game controller and poses him like an action figure. Jake is in his early forties, very fit, wearing a light blue oxford shirt, navy cashmere sweater, and well-tailored jeans.

Drew and Jake maintain intelligent but neutral expressions throughout.

Blackout.

In the darkness, we hear the sound of a video game. A video game announcer's voice says, "Get ready, fight!"

Lights up.

Jake is playing a video game on the sofa while Drew looks on. Silence while Jake plays and Drew watches.)

DREW *(Singing)*:

I'm a little airplane nyow
I'm a little airplane nyow nyow
I'm a little airplane nyow
I'm a little airplane nyow nyow
And wangity-wang, wangity-wang
I'm a little airplane nyow.

(Jake continues to play, ignoring Drew.

Drew stands behind Jake.

Drew sings again, this time louder. He makes a little airplane with his hand that he flies around Jake's face as he sings.)

I'm a little airplane nyow
I'm a little airplane nyow nyow
I'm a little airplane nyow
I'm a little airplane nyow nyow
And wangity-wang, wangity-wang
I'm a little airplane nyow.

(Jake continues to ignore Drew.
Drew taps Jake.)

I'm a little airplane.

JAKE: That song doesn't bother me anymore. I'm immune to it.
DREW: Oh.

(Drew sits down, then launches out of his chair to start singing
again, holding his arms out at his sides like airplane wings. As
he sings, he flies over to Jake and jumps onto the coffee table,
obstructing Jake's view of the TV with his wings.)

I'm a little airplane nyow
I'm a little airplane nyow nyow
I'm a little airplane nyow
I'm a little airplane nyow nyow
And wangity-wang, wangity-wang
I'm a little airplane nyow.

(He holds out his final "nyow," modulating his pitch higher as
he sits next to Jake on the sofa. Screaming:)

I'M—

(Jake attacks Drew. They struggle.)

Ow! Fuck!
JAKE: Are you gonna stop?
DREW: Jesus, yes!

(Jake releases him.)

JAKE *(Going back to his video game)*: You're a fucking idiot.

DREW: You're an idiot!

> *(Drew gets up and stands watching as Jake resumes his game.*
>
> *Drew jumps onto the couch and starts humping Jake's back while starting to sing again.*
>
> *Jake chases Drew, who taunts him from behind the recliner. They slap at each other. Jake chases Drew behind the sofa. They slap and kick at each other, then Jake wrestles Drew down to the ground.*
>
> *They struggle until Drew cries out in pain.)*

I'm done, I'm done!

Goddamn.

> *(Jake helps Drew up and slaps his ass. Drew massages his nipples [which Jake twisted when they were behind the sofa].)*

JAKE: Ready for a snack?

DREW: Go for it. I can't. I'm getting fat.

JAKE: What are you talking about, where?

DREW *(Pointing to his stomach)*: You don't know what shit looks like under here.

JAKE: You're crazy. *I'm* fat.

DREW: Dude, how are you fat? Don't you work out like six days a week?

JAKE: Yeah, but I use it as an excuse to eat everything I see. I've been eating so much this past week, you don't even know.

DREW: Oh I do know. I could go for some fucking Christmas cookies right now.

JAKE: Did Matt make his apple pie yet?

DREW: Can't touch it till tomorrow.

JAKE: I want it now!

DREW: Stop it, you're making me hungry!

JAKE: Come on, man, it's Christmas! We should be able to eat whatever the fuck we want!

DREW: Fuck it. Let's see what snacks Dad's got over there.
JAKE: Yeah!

(Drew runs over and opens the laundry closet, turning on a pull light to reveal a washer/dryer and wire shelves holding laundry supplies, board games, and jumbo barrels of snacks.)

DREW: Oh my god.
JAKE: What?
DREW: Privilege!

(Drew holds up a Monopoly game box with a large homemade label on top that reads: PRIVILEGE.)

JAKE: Oh my god.
DREW: The game where you have fun by not having fun!
JAKE: Wanna play?
DREW: Yeah.

(Drew grabs a jumbo barrel of snacks from the closet and brings it to the coffee table along with the game.

Jake opens the game box, revealing the inside of the lid, which has been decorated with a Black Power fist. Jake holds up the game board, revealing an anti-money symbol on one half and a female gender symbol on the other.)

JAKE *(Taking out a mints tin with the game pieces in it)*: I'm the iron!
DREW: Fuck!
JAKE: Ha ha! Undervalued domestic labor bonus!
DREW: Wait a minute, give me the thimble! That gets the bonus too!
JAKE: No it doesn't.
DREW: Bullshit. Let me see the rules.

(Drew grabs handwritten rules from the box, and shows Jake, who starts dealing out the money.)

See?

JAKE: Fine, you can have your domestic labor bonus.

(Drew sets up the cards and takes the thimble game piece.)

Roll to see who goes first.

(Drew picks up a die and thumps his head, pretending the die is falling out of his ear onto the board.
He gets a low number.)

Aww.

(Jake pretends to blow a die out of his nostril onto the board.
He gets a high number.)

Yes!

(Jake pretends to vomit the dice onto the board.
He moves his iron forward two spaces.)

Ugh, Excuses card.

DREW: Ha ha!

(Jake draws an "Excuses" [formerly "Community Chest"] card.)

JAKE *(Reading)*: "'What I said wasn't sexist-slash-racist-slash-homophobic because I was joking.' Pay fifty dollars to The Lesbian and Gay Community Services Center."

(Jake pays.
Drew mimes shitting the dice onto the floor.
Drew moves his thimble forward seven spaces.)

DREW: Shit!
JAKE: Denial card!

(Drew draws a "Denial" [formerly "Chance"] card.)

DREW *(Reading)*: "'I don't have white privilege because it doesn't exist.' Get stopped by the police for no reason and go directly to jail."

(Drew moves his thimble to the jail square.)

ED *(Offstage)*: Hello!

(Drew and Jake get up and move toward the door to the garage.)

DREW: Hey, finally!
JAKE: Hey!

(Drew and Jake exit into the garage.)

MATT AND JAKE *(Offstage, overlapping)*: Hey!
ED AND JAKE *(Offstage, overlapping)*: Hey!
JAKE *(Offstage, disappointed)*: Aw, man!
     Here Dad I got it.

(Matt enters backward, holding the bottom half of a giant arti-ficial Christmas tree by himself. He's in his mid-forties and handsome but badly dressed in baggy faded jeans, an oversized pale green button-up and a too-small brown fleece jacket. He also wears a big, worn-out coat and old snow boots.)

ED *(Offstage)*: Jake, you need help?

(Drew enters with three identically wrapped shoebox-sized boxes and puts them in the coat closet.)

JAKE *(Offstage)*: It's not that heavy, I'm fine.

(Jake enters backward, carrying the missing top half of the tree. Matt starts setting up the bottom half of the tree.

Ed, in his mid-seventies, enters, looking adorable in a red turtleneck, striped sweater, and tan corduroys. He also wears a jacket, cap, and boots. He carries a large bag from a discount chain store that he leaves by the mudroom.)

(Looking at the tree) Ugh. *(Handing the tree to Drew)* Here, take this thing!

(Drew takes the tree over to Matt and they finish setting it up.)

ED *(To Jake)*: Hey you!
JAKE: Hey Dad!
ED: Welcome home!

(Ed and Jake hug.)

You're looking well.
JAKE: You too.

(Ed takes off his coat, boots, and cap, and dons a pair of slippers.)

(Going to Matt) Hey, Big Brother.

(They hug.)

MATT: Hey. Nice to see you.

(Matt goes into the mudroom to take off his boots.)

JAKE *(Eyeing Matt's horrible outfit)*: Woo! You're looking slick!
MATT: Thanks. My stylist has been telling me to take more risks.

(Drew plugs in the tree. Only the bottom half of the lights come on.)

DREW: Ta-da!
ED: What the hell!
JAKE: Your fake tree is defective.
ED: It wasn't like that at the store!
MATT: Want me to take it back?
ED: No, it's almost dinnertime. We'll fix it.
JAKE: Why would you buy a fake tree?
ED: It was time.
JAKE: It's never time for a fake tree!
ED: That's a top-of-the-line tree!
JAKE: Really?
MATT: It was on sale because it was a display model.
JAKE: Of course it was.

(Drew starts pouring whiskeys.)

Why isn't the tree going in the living room?
ED: This is where we spend all our time now. What's the point of having a Christmas tree if you don't even see it?
JAKE: What's the point of having a Christmas tree if it's not a real tree?
ED: What's the point of having Christmas at all if you don't believe in Jesus?

JAKE: It's tradition!

MATT: Dad, I think we have to break it to him.

ED: Oh yeah.

JAKE: What.

ED: Jake, I'm not putting on the Santa suit this year.

(Jake looks disappointed. Drew stares at him.)

JAKE *(To Drew)*: What?

DREW: Oh my god! You want the Santa suit!

JAKE: No I don't!

DREW: Look at him! He looks like he's gonna cry!

MATT: I told you he'd be upset.

ED: I'm sorry, Jake, but without the kids here . . .

JAKE: I don't care!

ED: I could take you to the mall.

JAKE: Ha ha. Very funny.

DREW: Drinks!

(Drew hands everyone whiskeys.)

ED: Well. Here we are. Merry Christmas!

EVERYONE: Merry Christmas!

JAKE: What are we toasting to?

ED *(Turning toward the tree and holding up his glass)*: To the tree.

EVERYONE *(Turning toward the tree and holding up their glasses)*:
    To the tree!

ED: I'm glad to have you boys home.

(Matt notices the board game on the coffee table.)

MATT *(Going to look at it)*: Is that "Privilege"?

JAKE: Why yes it is.

ED: One of your mother's craftiest inventions.

(Ed goes over to the game.

Jake and Drew follow. Drew grabs the snack barrel and starts hogging it on the sofa.)

DREW: Remember when Mom made all our friends play it at Matt's birthday?

JAKE: No, it was Matt who made us.

ED: Well how else were you gonna learn not to be assholes?

DREW: How did you learn, Dad?

ED: It was a long and painful process. And I'm still an asshole.

JAKE: Speaking of assholes, how was Mrs. Johnson?

DREW: Did you fix her sink?

MATT: Dad did.

DREW: Who asks people over to fix their sink on Christmas Eve?

ED: It's a lonely time for her.

JAKE: Yeah, because she's a racist asshole.

ED: She grew up in a different time.

JAKE: That doesn't excuse what she said about April and the kids.

ED: Oh I know.

DREW: Does she know that interracial marriage is legal now?

JAKE: Dad, you didn't invite her to dinner, did you?

ED: I did!

JAKE: What?!

ED: Don't worry Jake, she's not coming.

JAKE: Oh my god. What, is she your girlfriend now?

ED *(Laughing)*: Oh, no.

JAKE: I don't know how you can stand to go over there.

ED: She has no one.

JAKE: Well, that's her fault.

ED: Sometimes you help people because they need help, and not because you like them.

DREW: Oh, you mean like when you have kids?

ED: How are the kids, Jake?

JAKE: Good. We did presents at their mom's before I flew out. Olivia says thank you for the chemistry set, and Miles says thanks for the Legos.

ED: Those are some good kids. Not like you boys.

DREW: Those little crackheads?

(Ed goes to get a bowl.)

ED: Olivia and Miles are crackheads?

DREW: Dad, you didn't know?

MATT: They're starting really early these days.

JAKE: Well, at least it's not affecting their schoolwork.

ED: Oh, they're young! Let 'em have their crack!

(He pours snacks from the jumbo container into the bowl. Matt takes the container from him and puts it back in the laundry closet. Drew grabs the bowl and resumes hogging the snacks.)

Drew, how do you like teaching?

DREW: I love it.

JAKE: Now that's a fucking scam. A full-time salary for one class!

DREW: It's a four-hour class!

ED: When is your novel coming out?

DREW: March.

MATT: The twentieth, right?

DREW: Yeah.

ED: How many awards is this one gonna win?

DREW: None. I'm tapped out.

ED: Will it be the same kind of thing? What did the *Times* critic call it? A "radical attack on the crassness of American materialism"?

DREW: No, I was thinking something more commercial. Maybe a memoir of my family trauma.

ED: Get me my whipping belt, Jake! Drew's gonna need some family trauma!

JAKE: Can you imagine Dad ever hitting anyone?

MATT: Only with his car.

ED: Hey, no jokes about my driving, it's Christmas Eve! And people who flunked driver's ed shouldn't talk.

JAKE: Matt only flunked driver's ed because he grabbed Mr. Rogalski's butt.

ED: That teacher who was touching all the girls? Didn't they fire that guy?

JAKE: Eventually, thanks to Matt.

DREW: The Teacher Terminator!

JAKE: That's right! Matt got the drama teacher fired for only casting white people in *Oklahoma!*

DREW: Oh my god. Matt and his friends showing up to opening night wearing KKK hoods singing that song!

JAKE *(Singing)*:
OOOO-klahoma.

(Drew joins in at "klahoma.")

JAKE AND DREW:
Where the wind comes sweepin' down the plain,

(Jake and Drew look to Matt for guidance in remembering the words and choreography. He joins in:)

MATT, JAKE AND DREW:
Where we sure look sweet, in white bed sheets,

(Bringing their arms up to a point above their heads.)

With our pointy masks upon our heads!

(Miming taking up rifles and loading them on the "k-k" sound, pronounced "kuh-kuh," and rhyming with the first syllable of "woman.")

OOOO-k-k-lahoma

(Scanning their imaginary rifles across the horizon and shooting.)

Ev'ry night my honey lamb and I,

(Making a "sitting and talking" pose and then a sweeping cross gesture with their arms.)

Sit alone and talk, and burn a cross

(Swinging their arms in circles above their heads as they stand up.)

While the smoke makes circles in the sky.

ED *(With showbiz flair, singing)*:
We know we belong to the Klan.

MATT, JAKE AND DREW *(Twirling imaginary lassos under their feet while skipping from side to side)*:
Yo-ho!

ED *(Singing)*:
And the Klan we belong to is grand!

MATT, JAKE AND DREW:
Yee-haw!

(Matt, Jake and Drew crack their imaginary lassos like whips as they replace the "Yee-haw!" of the original song with a whipping sound.)

(Singing, forming a single-file line and goose-stepping:)
And when we say,

(High-fiving each other with their Nazi salute hands.)

Yeeow!
Aye-yip-aye-yo-ee-ay!

(High-fiving each other with their Nazi salute hands.)

Yeeow!
We're only sayin'.

(Pointing at each other accusingly.)

You're really white, Oklahoma!
Oklahoma,

(Trying and failing to bounce up and down in a staggered rhythm on each "K.")

O.K.K.K.K.K.K.K.
OKLAHOMA,

(Making their bodies into "K" shapes.)

KKK!

DREW: I thought I was gonna die.
      (To Matt) Only you could have come up with that.
JAKE: That was fucking amazing.
ED: Matt was always trying to save the world.
MATT: Yeah, one ironically racist goose-step at a time.
DREW: Hey, that shit was hilarious.

MATT: Well, it was fun for us.

    Dad's been taking guitar lessons.

DREW: Really?

JAKE: Are you gonna play some Christmas songs for us?

ED: I'm learning "O Tannenbaum."

MATT: It's kind of amazing. He's been at it a month, but he sounds like he's never picked up a guitar in his life.

ED: Give me a break, I'm old! My mind doesn't retain things the way it used to.

MATT: Speaking of which, did you remember the check for Willy?

ED: Oh god, I forgot.

DREW: Who's Willy?

ED: The Fergus kid.

DREW: Oh, the genius from across the street?

ED: Well he's certainly not a genius at shoveling our driveway.

JAKE: You should make Matt do it.

ED: I wanted to give Willy a chance.

JAKE: Willy blew it! Next time don't hire a prodigy.

ED: Matt was a prodigy, and he never had any problems shoveling.

DREW: He would shovel for forty-eight hours straight.

JAKE: In a blizzard, with a broken leg—

ED: The hardest working kid I ever knew.

DREW: So what's it like living with this hardworking prodigy?

ED: It's been really wonderful. Unlike you boys, Matt pretends to care about my life.

MATT: No, I'm the kind of loser who finds you interesting.

ED: Hey, you're no loser. You do a lot.

    He does so much around the house I hardly have to lift a finger.

DREW *(To Matt)*: So what are you—you working on something?

ED: He works at a community organization.

MATT *(In a bragging voice)*: Yeah, at a temp job.

DREW: What? How did that happen?

ED: Your mom's friend Elaine works there.

MATT: Daddy got me the job!

JAKE: Dad and his girlfriends.

ED: Elaine is a married woman. And you boys talk an awful lot about girlfriends considering not one of you has one!

JAKE *(Laughing)*: I'm barely divorced, cut me some slack.

DREW: I have a girlfriend!

ED: For how long?

DREW: Two and a half months.

(Everyone laughs.)

JAKE: So you'll break up after New Year's, but before Valentine's Day.

ED: You wonder why I don't keep track. When I was growing up, everyone got married and stayed married. It was just what you did.

JAKE: Things are different now.

ED: Yeah, you young people think for yourselves. Back then, all we did was follow the rules.

DREW: What rules?

ED: Get a job, get married, buy a house, have kids.

DREW: Did you ever want anything different?

ED: It would never have even occurred to me to ask that question.

DREW: What do you mean?

ED: Unlike you boys, your mother and I didn't grow up being told we had any options. The only reason I even went to college was my school made me take the SAT, and I scored so high in science and math that the guidance counselor—

JAKE: There's no science in the SAT!

ED: Anyway, my guidance counselor told me I should go to school for engineering. And the field was booming, so that was that.

JAKE: But you worked your ass off too.

ED: Thank you, Son.

DREW: Do you feel like being an engineer was the best use of your abilities?

ED: I don't know. Probably not.

DREW: That's sad.

ED: Oh no, I've had a great life! I never dreamed I'd have all of this. I thought I'd end up like your Uncle Andrew.

DREW: Is he still driving the shuttle bus?

ED: Yeah, but it's been hard since he got sick.

(Pause.)

JAKE: So when's dinner coming?

MATT: Should be here soon, I ordered it for six o'clock.

JAKE: Jade Dragon?

MATT: Yeah.

DREW: So, Jake.

JAKE: What?

DREW: Are you excited?

JAKE: About what?

DREW: You know.

JAKE: What?

DREW: Someone you like is coming to town.

JAKE: Who?

MATT: Someone you *really* like.

ED: Your best friend.

JAKE: What are you guys talking about?

ED: You don't know him? He knows you. He knows when you are sleeping, he knows when you're awake—

(Matt, Drew and Ed crack up.)

JAKE: You're a bunch of fucking assholes.

ED: Oh, wait! I almost forgot!
    I'll be right back.
DREW: What's up?
ED *(Exiting)*: I have a surprise!
DREW *(To Matt)*: Do you know anything about this?
MATT: I do not.

(Jake takes a thick folder from the bookshelf and holds it up. It's labeled DREW'S WRITING in the same handwriting as was on the PRIVILEGE box.)

JAKE: Hey, guess what time it is?
MATT: I don't know. What time is it?
DREW: Oh Jesus.

(Jake takes a paper out of the folder.)

JAKE: It's time for a reading from Drew's early works!
DREW: Just do it, whatever.
JAKE *(Reading)*: "*Why I Hate People*, by Drew Norton. There are a lot of reasons why I hate people. The first reason is that they are boring. They talk and talk and talk about boring things nobody is interested in, and they have no idea how much they talk or how boring they are, because other people pretend to be interested. The second reason why I hate people is because they are stupid—"
DREW: Jake, you were actually the inspiration for all of that.
JAKE: God, you were such a little asshole.
MATT: Remember Drew's club? The "Fuck Humanity" club?
DREW: I seem to recall someone here starting his own school.
JAKE: You mean "Matt's School for Young Revolutionaries"?
MATT: Oh god.
JAKE: Good old SYR. Remember the uh . . . communist . . . uh, fight song?

(Jake and Drew do a sumo stomp.)

JAKE AND DREW *(Punching their chests with their right arms and extending them out)*: Ow!

(Chanting with accompanying militant arm gestures) "The individual's duty is to maintain the sovereignty of the state, at the risk and sacrifice of property and life."

(Punching their chests with their right arms and extending them out) Ow!

(Chanting with accompanying militant arm gestures) "Sacrifice on behalf of the state is the substantial tie between the state and all its members."

(They do an elaborate handshake, messing it up repeatedly until they finally get it right. Matt watches them from the sofa.)

DREW: How did Matt manage to get us to sit through SYR class every day?

(Drew and Jake go to Matt, attacking him with fight moves.)

JAKE: He taught us how to fight. And small-unit tactics. All the stuff a big brother's supposed to teach you.
DREW: Oh yeah. Where'd you learn all that stuff, Matt?
MATT: Who knows. Books.

(Matt jumps up off the sofa, karate-chopping at Jake and Drew's lower abdomens, and leaps over the coffee table, landing in a karate pose.)

JAKE: SYR class was awesome.
MATT: Awesomely Stalinist, apparently.
JAKE *(Grabbing Drew)*: Oh my god, remember when Shit-Baby cried?

MATT: Sorry Drew.

JAKE: He cried when we said he'd have to kill people when the revolution came.

(Matt and Drew attack each other.
Ed enters wearing red-and-green plaid pajamas. In his arms, he carries three sets of plaid pajamas, each in a different color, with ribbons tied around them.)

ED *(Holding up pajamas)*: Look at this!

DREW: Oh god, no.

ED: Yeah!

DREW: No!

ED: Christmas Eve pajamas! Remember Christmas Eve pajamas?

(He comes at Matt, Jake and Drew with the pajamas. Matt and Drew retreat, but Jake seems into it.)

MATT: Oh boy.

ED: Now put 'em on!

DREW: Yeah right.

(Ed throws pajamas at Jake, who catches them.)

JAKE: Okay.

(Jake starts taking off his pants.
Ed throws pajamas at Drew, who lets them hit his body and fall to the ground.)

ED *(Pointing at Drew)*: We're not eating without the pajamas!
(Noticing Jake with his pants down) Jake, you are not changing in my family room!

(Ed throws pajamas to Matt, who catches them.)

DREW: Are we doing this?

ED: Put 'em on!

MATT: Oh god.

ED *(Chasing Matt, Jake and Drew out of the room and shouting)*: Everyone put 'em on! Put on your pajamas!

(Matt, Jake and Drew exit.

Ed goes to the shopping bag he brought in earlier and brings it over to the fireplace.

He takes out a large box of candy canes and puts one in each of his son's stockings. He pulls out a large plastic bag of white tube socks and does the same thing. He pulls out a large pack of toothbrushes.)

JAKE *(From hallway)*: Here we come!

(Ed drops the toothbrushes back into the shopping bag.

While Matt makes an "oontz oontz oontz" dance beat noise, the brothers appear in the doorway one by one—first Drew, then Jake, then Matt—each striking an iconic male-model/boy-band-member pose.)

ED: Wow.

(Matt, Jake and Drew parade into the room like they're in a fashion show.)

DREW: What do you think?

ED: Terrific.

MATT: Do I look as good as I feel?

ED: You all look magnificent.

DREW: Does this color make my eyes pop?

JAKE: I'll make your eyes pop!

DREW: I'll make your— I'll piss on you!

(Drew pushes Jake into a chair and pretends to piss on him.)

I'll piss on your face!

JAKE *(Laughing)*: Stop it!

ED: What is this?

JAKE: Oh my god, Dad, I don't think we ever told you about this!

DREW: Do you know about when Matt pissed on Jake's friends?

ED: When was this?

DREW: High school. Matt got mad because Jake and his friends were playing "Gay Chicken."

ED: What's "Gay Chicken"?

DREW: It's where straight guys dare each other to do shit like, I don't know, put their balls on each other's faces, and whoever chickens out first, loses.

ED: Sounds like a fun game.

DREW: Anyway, Matt of course found this to be totally offensive, so he asked if he could play, took out his dick, and pissed all over Jake and his friends!

MATT: Sorry Jake.

JAKE: No, everything about that was genius.

DREW: Yeah Matt, you're a fucking genius.

MATT: For what, whipping out my dick?

ED: You were always such a socially conscious kid.

MATT *(To Jake)*: Sorry.

JAKE: A man with a dick like yours never needs to apologize.

DREW: Yeah, Matt. Stop being so self-deprecating.

(Pause.)

JAKE: So what do you guys do for fun around here? You two hit the bars?

ED: We hit the bars in the bathroom.

(Nobody knows what he's talking about.)

The bathroom . . . towel bars!

(Matt abruptly exits.)

DREW: Where'd he go?

JAKE: Dad's bad sense of humor scared him away.

DREW: Your face scared him away.

JAKE: Oh yeah? Your face is . . . also scared him away, because—

ED: Boys, boys! Let's try to have a civilized discussion.

JAKE: Okay, Dad. What would you like to discuss? Politics, religion—

ED: I'm thinking of buying a new car.

JAKE: Already? The Honda's only twenty years old!

ED: The Honda's fine. But I'm old, I wanna treat myself.

JAKE: Well good for you! What are you thinking of getting?

ED: Your Aunt Janet is selling her BMW.

JAKE: Wow Dad.

DREW: You can't get a BMW.

ED: Why not?

DREW: BMW is a rich jerkoff banker car. Jake drives a BMW.

(Jake flips Drew off.
  The doorbell rings.)

JAKE: Finally.

MATT *(From offstage)*: I'll get it.

DREW *(Picking up empty glasses and the snack bowl)*: I'll get some plates.

(Drew exits.)

JAKE: God, I'm hungry.

ED: Let's pull the table a little closer.

(Jake and Ed pull the table closer to the sofa and start clearing it off.)

I always love Jade Dragon. You remember the Kims?

JAKE: Sure.

ED: They're building a giant new house on the hill.

(Drew reenters with plates and a six-pack of beer.)

JAKE: Wow, the restaurant must be doing well.

(Matt enters with a bag of Chinese food and sits with Ed and Jake on the sofa.)

ED: It's always packed in there. They had to expand it.

(Drew sets the plates and beer on the coffee table and Jake starts distributing plates.
    Drew starts to sit in a chair while looking at his phone.)

(To Drew) Where do you think you're going?

DREW *(Looking at Ed, Matt and Jake on the sofa)*: We can't do that anymore, Dad! We're too big!

(Matt takes utensils and napkins out of the bag.)

ED: Nonsense, we'll all squeeze in!

DREW: Come on, Dad.

JAKE *(Patting a spot next to him)*: Drew, here's your spot right here.

DREW: Oh my god.

(Drew squeezes between Jake and Matt on the sofa, still looking at his phone. Jake starts distributing utensils. Everyone gets chopsticks except for Ed, who gets a fork. Matt starts taking Chinese food out of the bag.)

ED: Oh, this is great!

JAKE *(To Drew)*: Put away your phone, jackass, we're about to eat.

DREW: I'm writing a student.

ED: On Christmas Eve?

DREW: He's Jewish.

JAKE: Stop working, it's Christmas.

ED: All right, let's eat.

(Ed and Jake start helping themselves. Drew opens a container, grabs a pot sticker with his fingers, and eats it.)

DREW: Oh my god. So good.

JAKE: Shit-Baby loves Jade Dragon!

ED: What is "Shit-Baby"?

JAKE: That's what we called Drew.

DREW: My whole childhood.

ED: They called you "Shit-Baby"? I never knew.

That was mean of you boys!

JAKE: Remember when we made Shit-Baby eat his own shit?

DREW: I was three.

ED: You made him eat his own shit? That's horrible!

JAKE: It all comes out on Christmas!

DREW: Can we please talk about something other than me eating my own shit at the dinner table?

ED: I'm going to Nova Scotia for my cruise this year.

DREW: Again? For the puffins?

JAKE: Dad, you're obsessed!

ED: I am not obsessed with puffins!

DREW: Yes you are! You're obsessed with them!

ED: Define "obsessed."

JAKE: Dad, you have puffin paraphernalia, you wear socks with puffins on them—

DREW: You went to Northumberland for a puffin festival!

ED: So?

JAKE: So, that's an obsession!

ED: The puffin is a wonderful animal! Very sociable.

DREW *(Holding up a piece of meat with his chopsticks)*: Tastes pretty good too.

ED: What?

JAKE: Dad, don't you like your General Tso's Puffin?

ED: I'm worried about you boys. You're not funny.

DREW: Hey Matt, you want some Puffin Fried Rice?

MATT: Yeah. Sorry.

JAKE: Here, have a Puffin Pot Sticker.

DREW: Where's your usual, Matt?

MATT: Sorry, what?

DREW: Where's your Moo Shu Puffin?

ED: Here, have some of this.

MATT *(Trying not to cry)*: Yeah.

DREW: Are you okay?

MATT: I'm fine.

JAKE: What's wrong?

ED: Are you sick?

MATT: I'll be fine.

ED *(Getting up and going to Matt)*: Hey, hey hey hey hey.

(Ed sits next to Matt on the arm of the sofa, putting his arm around him. Matt starts to cry.)

MATT: I'm sorry.

JAKE: Hey, don't worry.

DREW: It's okay. What's going on, man? Do you wanna talk about it?

ED: Take a second.

MATT: I'm sorry.

DREW: Man, it's okay.

(Matt tries to get up.)

JAKE: No no, we'll go.

DREW: Matt—

JAKE: I think we should give the guy some space.

(Jake gets up to leave, tapping Drew on the shoulder.)

ED: He just needs a second.

DREW: Matt, do you want—

ED: He'll be okay.

(Jake impatiently slaps Drew's shoulder.
Blackout.)

TRANSITION ONE

Lights up as "O Holy Night" plays.

The People in Charge enter with two Stagehands (preferably female) dressed in black. They oversee the Stagehands as the latter carefully and methodically prepare the stage for the next act.

When the Stagehands are done with their work, the People in Charge bring Jake and Drew onstage and put them into position, posing them like action figures.

Blackout.

ACT TWO

Lights up on Jake and Drew trying to fix the Christmas tree lights. Jake is wearing his Santa suit and slippers. Drew is wearing dark skinny jeans, a denim work shirt, patterned socks, and identical slippers to Jake's, which are the same as the ones Ed was wearing in Act One. (Ed bought all his sons slippers for Christmas.)

"O Holy Night" plays on the stereo while they work on the lights. The Christmas tree lights flicker and then come on.

JAKE: Hey!

(They high-five.)

Okay, now we can decorate it!

(They pick up strands of popcorn from a plastic bin.)

(Going to stereo) Hey.

DREW: What?
JAKE *(Turning off stereo)*: Peter Piper.
DREW: Oh shit.

> *(Jake and Drew rap the opening lines of Run-DMC's "Peter Piper" in tandem. They do it in a dorky way, making no effort to sound or look like rappers. [That is, no "rap hand gestures," please.])*

JAKE: Nowww Peter
DREW: Piper
JAKE: Picked
DREW: Peppers
JAKE: But Run rocked
DREW: Rhymes
JAKE: Humpty
DREW: Dumpty
JAKE: Fell
DREW: Down
JAKE: That's his hard
DREW: Time.
JAKE: Jack B.
DREW: Nimble
JAKE: What
DREW: Nimble
JAKE: And he was
DREW: Quick
JAKE: But Jam
DREW: Master
JAKE: Cut
DREW: Faster
JAKE AND DREW: Jack's on Jay's dick.

> *(They sing the song's instrumental break, replicating it exactly.)*

DREW: Do you remember when Mom played that song one time when she made us dance together after we fought?

JAKE: Yeah, Mom's "dance parties."

DREW: Oh, that was the worst.

(They start putting their popcorn strands on the tree. Jake winds his carefully around the tree, while Drew messily arranges his on one side.

Jake looks at Drew's popcorn strands.)

JAKE: What are you doing?

DREW: What.

JAKE: You should be going *around* the tree.

DREW: Relax, man.

JAKE: You're clumping them!

DREW: No I'm not!

JAKE: You're making it look bad!

(Jake yanks Drew's popcorn strands off the tree and starts redoing them.)

We should just go eat that fucking pie.

DREW: Matt said hands off.

(Pause.)

Listen man, I think Matt's clinically depressed.

JAKE: What?

DREW: He started crying in the middle of dinner! Why are you pretending like it didn't happen?

JAKE: He said it was nothing.

DREW: And you believed him?

JAKE: Matt doesn't lie.

DREW: What does the guy have to do, slit his wrists in front of you?

JAKE: Stop being dramatic.

DREW: Matt was valedictorian. He went to Harvard. And now he's making copies and living with Dad.

JAKE: Trust me, Drew. Matt's fine.

DREW: When's the last time that guy had a girlfriend?

JAKE: I don't know.

DREW: I don't think he dates anymore, like, at all. I don't understand that. He's funny, he's good-looking.

I tried to get him to come out to me once.

JAKE: What? Are you crazy?

DREW: I know! If Matt were gay, he'd be leading the pride parade.

JAKE: No way. Pride's too corporate for Matt.

DREW: Yeah, true.

I don't understand what his problem is.

JAKE: Drew, can you please just give it a rest? We can talk about Matt after Christmas. Just let me enjoy this.

DREW: Fine.

(Pause.)

JAKE: I can't believe I broke the [name of video game console].

DREW: You shouldn't slam the controller down every time you lose.

JAKE: No, I shouldn't lose.

(Ed and Matt enter from the garage.

Ed is wearing green corduroys, a red cardigan, and a plaid shirt, with his coat, boots, and cap.

Matt is wearing the same ill-fitting jeans from the day before, with a baggy tan button-up shirt that makes him blend into the similarly colored furniture. He also wears his coat and boots.)

ED: Hey, you fixed the lights!
DREW: Yeah.

(The following joking exchange should have the desperate tone of two people panicking over how to disarm a nuclear bomb.)

JAKE *(Running over to Matt and grabbing him)*: PIE!
MATT: I'll grab it!
JAKE: Is there whipped cream?
MATT: Yeah, but I'm gonna have to whip it!
JAKE: Then go do that!
MATT: Okay, I will!

(Matt runs panicking toward the kitchen but suddenly stops and starts running in slow motion. Jake shoves him out of the room.
Jake goes to Ed.)

JAKE: That was fast. How was Mrs. Johnson?
ED: Not in the best mood. She would barely open her door.
JAKE: Did you manage to get the cookies in?
ED: Just barely.

(Drew approaches Ed.)

DREW: Did Matt say anything?
ED: About what?
DREW: About last night.
ED: Oh, no.
DREW: That's weird.
ED: He's fine.
JAKE: Dad, I think I broke your Christmas present.
ED: What?

(Jake holds up the video game controller.)

JAKE: I dropped your controller.

ED: That was a gift for me?

JAKE: Yeah, I forgot to tell you. I opened it early for you.

ED: Oh!

JAKE: Whoops.

ED: I never even got a chance to play it!

JAKE: It's the thought that counts.

ED: Well, thank you, Son.

> *(From offstage, Matt makes the whistling noise and "wah wah wah" sound from the* The Good, the Bad and the Ugly *theme song.*
>
> *Matt enters with a pie and four forks, walking like a cowboy. He jangles the forks together in his hand with each step to simulate the sound of spurs. He stops in a cowboy pose.)*

MATT *(Cowboy voice)*: Pie.

> *(Jake spits imaginary tobacco juice.)*

JAKE *(Cowboy voice, his hand on an imaginary gun)*: Where's the whipped cream?

MATT *(Cowboy voice)*: Sorry, there wasn't enough.

JAKE *(Cowboy voice)*: You motherfucker!

> *(Jake starts to draw his gun.*
>
> *Drew makes a loud whinnying noise as he rears an imaginary horse. He makes galloping-hooves noises as he rides his horse, shooting at Jake and Matt as he goes.*
>
> *Jake and Matt stare at him as if that's the lamest thing they've ever seen in their lives.)*

Drew sullenly grabs the pie and puts it on the table as Matt hands out forks.

Ed, Drew, Jake and Matt all dig into the pie with their forks simultaneously.)

So Dad, are you still doing yoga?

ED: No, I gave that up.

JAKE: Good, that shit'll fuck you up.

ED: Matt and I have been so busy.

JAKE: With what? Hanging out with old ladies?

ED: We've had so many projects around the house. And we've been watching movies.

MATT: We should all watch a movie tomorrow.

ED: That's a good idea!

MATT: I'll pick one up when I go to the store.

ED: That would be great.

JAKE: Dad, you got your buddy back. Must be nice having someone around the house again.

ED: It really is. It's hard living alone when you're not used to it.

JAKE: Yeah, I hear you.

ED: I had your mother for so long.

JAKE: You've been such a soldier about it.

ED: Not really. I was in bad shape for a long time.

DREW: Have you ever thought about seeing someone?

ED: Again with the girlfriends!

DREW: No, I meant like a therapist.

ED: A therapist?

DREW: I've been seeing one for a few years now, and it's helped a lot.

ED: With what? Are you all right?

DREW: Yeah, never better. But you guys remember how fucked-up I used to be. My whole life—all that negativity.

ED: I remember those essays you used to write for school.

DREW: Yeah, it's amazing how much talking helped.

(Pause.)

Matt, have you ever thought about trying therapy, or . . . ?

MATT: Um, for what?

DREW: Uh . . .

JAKE: So, what movie are we gonna watch tomorrow?

ED: Good question.

JAKE: Horror movie?

ED: No horror. The older I get, the less I want to see terrible things.

JAKE: Action?

MATT: Eh.

JAKE: Too stereotypical?

DREW: Matt, I didn't mean—

MATT: Everything's cool, Drew.

DREW: Is it?

MATT: Yeah.

(Matt gets up.)

DREW: Matt—

MATT: Eggnog.

(Matt exits.)

DREW: Shit!

JAKE: So Dad, how do you like the new coach of the—

DREW: Jake!

JAKE: What.

DREW: You keep . . .

JAKE: I keep what?

DREW: You're acting like you don't give a shit!

JAKE: About what, Matt? Of course I do!

DREW: Doesn't seem like it!

JAKE: Just leave the poor guy alone.
DREW: Why?
JAKE: Because it's what he wants.
DREW: That's, like . . . cowardly macho bullshit!

(Matt enters and overhears the following:)

JAKE: I'm not the one freaking out that a dude cried!
ED: Boys, boys!

(Matt approaches with a crystal punch bowl of eggnog and matching glasses.)

Thank you, Matt!
MATT: No problem.

(Silence as Matt pours eggnog.)

ED *(Taking cup)*: Oh, thank you. *(Sipping)* Mmm.
DREW *(Taking cup)*: Thanks, Matt.
JAKE *(Taking cup, simperingly)*: Why thank you!
ED: Matt, this is great!
MATT: Thanks. I poured it out of a carton.
ED: Very good!
You didn't put any spices in it?
MATT: No.
ED: Well, it tastes wonderful!
JAKE *(Simperingly)*: It really does!
MATT: I'm glad.

(Pause.)

ED *(To Matt)*: I wrote the check for Willy. It's on the desk.
MATT: Great. I'll give it to him on Tuesday.

ED: Thanks, Son.

MATT: We never decided on a movie.

JAKE: That's right!

MATT: Jake wants an action movie.

JAKE: Yeah!

ED: So let's get an action movie for Jake!

(Ed reaches for a bowl of chips and spills them on the floor.)

Shit!

MATT *(Jumping up)*: I got it.

ED: Thank you, Matt.

(Matt scoops chips back into the bowl and exits.)

DREW: Come on!

ED: Can we please just try to have a nice evening?

JAKE: Sounds good to me.

DREW: How can we have a nice evening when Matt is fucking miserable?

JAKE: What makes you think he's miserable?

DREW: He cried! In the middle of dinner! Why'd he do that?

JAKE: Well, all we did last night was harp on his high school glory days like we think he's some sort of washout now. I can see how that would get old.

ED: I think it's his financial situation. It must be weighing on him.

DREW: What financial situation?

ED: His student loans are killing him. I think that's why he moved back here, so he could pay them off.

DREW: How long is he planning to stay here?

ED: We haven't really discussed it.

DREW: Dad!

JAKE: Dad, I think it's great.

DREW: You think it's great for Matt to live with Dad forever?

ED: Who said anything about forever?

JAKE: Dad, you like having Matt here, right?

ED: Of course, it's been wonderful.

JAKE: And you feel like Matt's okay with it?

ED: I haven't seen him this cheerful in years.

JAKE: So what's the problem?

DREW: Dad, I know you like having Matt around, and I'm sure on some level he feels comfortable here, but he deserves to have his own life!

JAKE: What's wrong with what he's doing? In some cultures, Matt would be revered for taking care of Dad!

ED: I'm not quite in need of a caretaker yet!

DREW: Exactly! Dad doesn't even need him here! Matt should be doing something more than this!

JAKE: He's helping groups that support . . . oppressed people.

DREW: Yeah, he's "helping" by making copies as an office . . . lackey! It's depressing! He could be running those places!

ED: Oh, of course!

JAKE: Matt doesn't want to be some big hotshot!

DREW: Yeah, because he has low self-esteem!

JAKE: That's not the reason! He's making a choice! Just because all we care about is our own success doesn't mean Matt has to!

(Matt enters with a vacuum cleaner.)

DREW: That's not all I care about!

JAKE: Of course it is! That's why you're so obsessed with therapy!

DREW: What's wrong with—

(Matt starts vacuuming potato chip crumbs. He is thorough and it takes a long time. Ed watches Matt vacuuming and lifts

> *his feet up so Matt can vacuum under them. Matt finishes by*
> *using the hose attachment to get the last of the crumbs.*
> *Matt turns off the vacuum.)*

ED: Thank you, Son.

MATT: No problem.

DREW *(To Jake)*: What's wrong with therapy?

JAKE: Nothing. It's great for guys like you and me. The whole point of therapy is to help us get out there, climbing the ladder and selling ourselves, even when times get tough.

DREW: The point of therapy is to learn how to be happy!

JAKE: Yeah, because unhappiness doesn't sell! People hate losers!

DREW: Matt, I know you think therapy is bullshit, I get it, but—

MATT: I don't think therapy is bullshit.

DREW: So you're open to the idea?

(Drew goes to Matt.)

Matt, what the hell happened last night? Why did you cry?

MATT: I don't think this is gonna be a good conversation.

ED: Was it because of your financial situation?

MATT: No, Dad.

JAKE: God, why can't a guy fucking cry if he wants?

DREW: Guys can cry, but if they're unhappy, then they need—

JAKE: Why does everyone have to be happy? What if that's not what's important to them?

DREW: Who doesn't want to be happy?

JAKE: Matt!

DREW: Matt, do you want to be happy?

MATT: I don't know. I'm not sure what you mean.

JAKE: See? His mind doesn't even work that way! Why does he have to be selfish and only focus on his own happiness?

DREW: It's not selfish to focus on your own happiness! I know this may be hard for you to grasp, but my happiness comes from using my abilities in service to something bigger than myself.

JAKE: Oh yeah? And who are you serving?

DREW: My community. You know, my readers, my students.

JAKE: Come on, Drew! How is being another white guy with tenure making a difference?

DREW: What does being white have to do with it?

JAKE: For Matt, everything! Our success is a problem, not a solution!

ED: What are you boys talking about? What does any of this have to do with Matt?

JAKE: Okay, Dad. Why does Drew think that Matt needs to be a big hotshot? Because Matt's smart, right? Okay, so why is he smart?

ED: Because he got his brains from his mother.

DREW: Don't sell yourself short, Dad.

JAKE: Matt has brains, but more importantly, he got an incredible education. You made enough money to live in a good school district, so Matt got to have great teachers and all this support.

ED: Matt also worked very hard.

JAKE: But working hard was all he ever had to worry about! He never had to worry about having enough food or getting shot. It was easier for him to climb the ladder because he was born with every advantage. No one ever assumed he was stupid because he was a woman or stopped his car because he was Black. The system is rigged.

Remember that rule in Privilege where you'd lose money for being white when you pass go?

ED: I never liked that rule.

JAKE: Well, that's what Matt's trying to do. He's penalizing himself!

MATT: That's not what I'm doing.

JAKE: Yes you are! You're deferring to people who don't have your unfair advantages!

DREW: So, white guilt? The reason Matt hates himself is because he's a white guy?

JAKE: He doesn't hate himself, moron!

MATT: Guys, come on!

JAKE: Matt, do you hate yourself?

MATT: No.

JAKE: See?

DREW: Matt, do you believe that you deserve to be punished for being a white guy?

MATT: No!

ED: Okay, Matt has said no. And anyway, Jake, all your stuff about race is ludicrous.

JAKE: Why is it ludicrous?

ED: You don't even believe it yourself!

JAKE: Yes I do! White guys like us shouldn't be running things.

ED: Skin color shouldn't have anything to do with it! What we need is a level playing field.

JAKE: Dad, when it comes to capitalism, there's no such thing as a level playing field.

ED: Oh, don't start with the socialism, Jake. You're a banker!

JAKE: Hey, I'm not the only hypocrite in this family!

MATT: Guys, can we drop this?

DREW: No! We've been letting this go on long enough! Dad, it's selfish of you to let Matt stay here.

MATT: What?!

DREW: I'm sorry, Matt, but you need to go out and fulfill your potential.

MATT: Drew, stop!

JAKE: But that's not what Matt's about! He cares about doing the right thing. It's the rest of us who are choosing to be assholes!

ED: Wait a minute, how am I choosing to be an asshole?

JAKE: By using up resources, taking up space, enjoying your privilege.

ED: You mean by living on this earth?

I also vote, I give to charity, I volunteer . . .

JAKE: Yeah, but you're doing all that from inside an unfair system that benefits you!

ED: Jake, this is nonsense!

JAKE: It's what you and Mom taught us!

ED: We never taught you this!

JAKE: Sure you did!

ED: That's nonsense Jake!

JAKE: You taught us to obsess over privilege!

ED: Your mother and I taught you to appreciate what you have. Do some good with it. Not sit around talking about it for the sake of talking!

DREW: Yeah Jake, you sound like an undergrad.

JAKE: Oh, you're so smart? What are your answers?! Your socially aware novels, Dad's checkbook activism?

MATT: Jake, stop.

JAKE: What! I'm trying to get them to understand where you're coming from!

MATT: I know, but—

ED: You're talking nonsense!

JAKE: Matt's actually making the sacrifice! He's trying not to take up space!

MATT: No I'm not!

JAKE: Admit it! You're making yourself invisible the way you think we're supposed to!

ED: Nonsense, nonsense, nonsense—

JAKE: Dad shut—

DREW: Oh my god.

(Pause.)

ED: Jake, you don't tell me to shut up in my house.

(Ed gets up.)

I'm going to bed.

JAKE: Dad.

ED: Good night. *(Pausing in the doorway)*
    Merry Christmas.

(He exits.)

DREW *(Picking up the forks and pie plate)*: I'm out.

MATT *(Picking up the eggnog bowl and glasses)*: Me too.

JAKE: Guys, come on.

MATT *(Exiting)*: Sorry, Jake.

DREW *(Turning the lights off on Jake as he exits)*: Nice work, jackass!

JAKE: Fuck off, Drew!
    (Shouting into the hallway) Fine, go!
    I've been carrying this whole team on my back all Christmas!

(Jake angrily yanks off his Santa suit and slippers and hurls them into the laundry room. He is wearing dark jeans and a blue button-down shirt.)

(Shouting into the hallway) I'm putting on some Christmas carols!

(Jake hooks his phone up to the stereo and starts playing an upbeat, high-tempo pop song, featuring women singing together. He looks at the doorway.
    He turns the music up and checks the doorway again.

He pours himself a whiskey, downing it in one shot.

Jake starts to dance frenetically. He gets increasingly into it, gyrating his hips lasciviously.

Drew enters.)

DREW: Jake what the fuck are you doing?

(Jake turns and dances toward Drew. When Drew doesn't respond, Jake makes a pleading "come on" gesture.

Drew suddenly bursts into a frantic sideways dance. He somersaults over the sofa.

They dance to the front of the sofa, pushing the coffee table closer to the sofa to make more room to dance.

They dance ridiculously, mirroring each other. They do a hip-hop dance move, poorly. They do a coordinated hoedown move that culminates in Jake bending Drew over and humping him from behind. When Drew realizes what's happening, he cheerfully dances along.

Matt and Ed enter.

Jake goes over to Ed and freaks him against the bathroom door. Drew does a Michael Jackson–impersonating dance across the room.

Jake dances frenetically toward Matt and forces him to dance by grabbing his arms and waving them in the air. Jake lets go and Matt starts miming spinning records like a deejay.

Jake and Drew do the robot, which turns into being zombies. They walk over to Matt as zombies and attack him behind the sofa.

Matt bursts up from behind the sofa as a zombie, and Jake and Drew run away.

Ed claps his hands and shouts, "Hey!" from the doorway to get their attention. He does a little dance in the doorway.

Jake and Drew drag a resisting Matt into the room and abandon him there, waiting expectantly. Matt bursts into an

*epic, impressively athletic solo dance. At one point, Matt pretends
to rip Jake's heart out of his chest,* Indiana Jones*–style.*
    They all dance as the lights fade.
    Blackout.)

TRANSITION TWO

The music segues into an upbeat instrumental pop track.

Lights up.

The People in Charge return to the stage with the Stagehands, who set the stage for the next act.

When the Stagehands are done, the People in Charge put Drew into position lying asleep on the sofa. Person in Charge 1 drapes a blanket over him. Person in Charge 2 adjusts Drew's mouth so that it hangs open.

Blackout.

ACT THREE

Bright morning lights up on Drew asleep on the sofa, wearing the same clothes from the night before.

Matt is picking up empty beer bottles and glasses, trying to be as quiet as possible. He's wearing the same bad jeans and another baggy tan button-up.

Matt brings the bottles and glasses into the kitchen, and returns with some wood-cleaner spray, a rag, and a wastebasket. He sprays the table down and wipes it with the rag, sweeping crumbs into the wastebasket. He exits.

Jake enters from the garage, slamming the door behind him. He's wearing several layers of expensive running gear.

Jake opens the half-bathroom door, revealing pink floral wallpaper, and removes some of his running gear. He grabs a small pink embroidered hand towel, which he uses to wipe his underarms.

Jake approaches the sleeping Drew and places the towel over his mouth. He presses down until Drew starts to suffocate and wakes with a muffled yell.

DREW: Fuck! Oh.

JAKE: Good morning.

DREW: What time is it?

JAKE: Ten.

DREW: Wait, um. What's going on?

JAKE: I went for a run.

DREW: You went for a run?

JAKE: You should get some water.

DREW: What happened?

JAKE: We got drunk.

DREW: How did you go for a run? What the fuck are you doing?

JAKE *(Taking a one-handed selfie with his phone)*: Self-actualizing.

DREW *(Sitting up)*: It's not fair. You drank like five times as much as I did. I feel like I'm gonna die. Jesus.

(Matt enters.)

MATT: Morning!

JAKE: Morning! How goes it?

MATT: Good, how was your run?

JAKE: Great.

DREW: Am I the only one who's—I feel like I'm gonna die.

JAKE: Did you get the bagels?

MATT: Yeah, they're in the kitchen.

DREW: Oh, fuck. Why didn't you wake me up?

JAKE: You looked so sweet.

MATT: Drew.

(Drew looks at Matt. Matt's eyes roll into the back of his head as he transforms into "Pterodactyl Man.")

DREW: Oh no. Not this.

(Matt makes a loud screeching noise and perches imaginary claws on Drew's head with a squawk.)

MATT *(Screeching into Drew's ear)*: Want some coffee?

DREW: Some water would be great.

MATT *(Screeching)*: Great!

DREW: Goddamn it.

(Matt exits with a loud screeching cry, flapping his pterodactyl wings.)

I know it sounds like I'm joking, but I really feel like I'm actually gonna die.

JAKE: You used to be so into dying. Remember when you dug your own grave in the backyard?

DREW: Is it still there? I'm fucking ready.

(Matt reenters as Pterodactyl Man. He climbs up onto the back of the sofa, shoving a full glass of water at Drew and perching his claws on Drew's head with a squawk.)

MATT *(Screeching)*: Drew! Here's your water!

(Drew takes a sip of water.)

(Screeching) How's it taste?

DREW: Fine.

MATT *(Screeching)*: Good!

DREW *(Shoving Matt off the sofa so that he falls behind it)*: Stop it!
      (Turning to Jake) Anyway—

(Jake leaps up onto the couch as "Monster Baby Man," pawing at Drew.)

JAKE *(Bellowing)*: What's wrong?

MATT *(Leaping onto the sofa back and screeching)*: What's wrong with your water, Drew?

JAKE *(Bellowing)*: Don't you like how it tastes?

MATT *(Screeching)*: Does your water taste nice, Drew?

DREW: You don't wanna start these games with me right now!

JAKE *(Bellowing)*: What games?

MATT *(Screeching)*: What games?

JAKE *(Bellowing)*: Don't you like your water, Drew?

DREW: Yes!

MATT *(Screeching)*: Do you want another glass?

JAKE *(Bellowing)*: Come on, let's get Drew another glass of water!

> *(Matt and Jake exit noisily into the hallway and continue to make loud, monstrous noises from the kitchen.*
>
> *Drew puts his water on the table with a pained expression.*
>
> *Jake and Matt reenter, each holding a glass of water. As they approach Drew, they emit sustained loud noises that cut off abruptly as they arrive behind Drew's head. They each hold a glass over one of Drew's shoulders, hovering over him.)*

MATT *(In the voice of the Templar Knight guarding the Holy Grail in* Indiana Jones and the Last Crusade*)*: You can only choose one.

> *(Drew contemplates the glasses.)*

DREW: I choose . . .

> *(He grabs the glasses and throws the water in Matt and Jake's faces.)*

MATT: Wrong choice!

JAKE: You're dead!

> *(Matt grabs Drew's first glass of water off the coffee table as Jake tackles Drew on the sofa.)*

DREW: Wait wait wait wait wait!

JAKE: Just let it happen.

(Jake holds Drew down while Matt pours the entire glass of water on Drew's face.)

DREW: Oh fuck.

(Matt and Jake let Drew up.)

You fuckers.

(Jake goes to the laundry closet and starts taking off his wet shirt.)

MATT *(Walking toward the laundry closet)*: You guys want some bagels?

JAKE: Yeah!

MATT: Drew, I'll bring you a towel.

DREW: Did you get Hoffman's?

(Jake hands Matt two towels from the dryer and starts changing into a sleek black T-shirt.)

MATT: Hoffman's was closed. I had to go to Nature Market.

DREW: Ugh! Nature Market bagels taste like Canadian bagels!

MATT: Do you want one or not?

(Matt throws Drew a tiny pink washcloth.)

DREW: I want Hoffman's!

MATT: I know you do, Shit-Baby, but I couldn't get them today. I'll get some tomorrow.

DREW *(Screaming and kicking in a tantrum)*: NOOO!

(Matt changes into a baggy mustard-colored T-shirt.

Jake starts making kung fu–movie fighting noises and wielding a towel like nunchucks.)

JAKE *(Attacking Drew with his towel, moving his mouth as if the words were dubbed in a kung fu movie)*: Stop acting like a baby, Shit-Baby!

DREW: Shut up.

(Drew curls up in the easy chair, placing his tiny pink washcloth over his knee, as if covering himself with a blanket.)

MATT: I'll get the bagels.

JAKE: No, I'll do it. You've been doing everything.

(Jake exits. Matt dries off the sofa and surrounding furniture with a towel. He places pillows back on the sofa. He grabs the Christmas blanket to throw in the washing machine. He brings Drew a large, baby blue towel and covers him with it. Drew flings his tiny pink washcloth to the floor.)

DREW: Will you read me a story?

MATT: You're feeling that bad?

DREW: Yes.

MATT: What story do you want?

DREW: Um. Silenus.

MATT: Okay.

(Matt goes over to the bookshelf and takes out Nietzsche's The Birth of Tragedy.*)*

Bookmark's still there.

(Matt sits and reads as if reading a fairy tale to a child:)

"According to the old story, King Midas had long hunted wise Silenus, Dionysus's companion, without catching him. When Silenus had finally fallen into his clutches, the king asked him what was the best and most desirable thing of all for mankind. The daemon stood silent, stiff and motionless, until at last, forced by the king, he gave a shrill laugh and spoke these words: 'Miserable, ephemeral race, children of hazard and hardship, why do you force me to say what it would be much more fruitful for you not to hear? The best of all things is something entirely outside your grasp: not to be born, not to be, to be nothing. But the second-best thing for you—is to die soon.'"

(Drew's eyes are closed.
Jake reenters with bagels.)

JAKE *(Bellowing)*: Bagels! *(In normal voice)* Aww. Shit-Baby's sleeping.

(Jake pushes Drew's nose with his foot, waking him.
Drew gets up, goes to the laundry closet, and changes from his wet shirt into the red plaid shirt he was wearing in Act One.
Matt snatches the plate of bagels from Jake.)

Hey!

MATT *(Holding the bagels out of Jake's reach)*: What's the passcode?

JAKE: Gimme a fucking bagel, Matt!

MATT: Tina Turner Tina Turner Tina Turner. Say it.

JAKE: Come on, man.

MATT: You have to say it correctly.

JAKE: Tina Turner Tina Turner Tina Turner.

MATT: Wrong! *(Saying it in a different way)* It's "Tina Turner Tina Turner Tina Turner."

JAKE: Stop being an asshole!

(He reaches for the bagels. Matt runs away.)

MATT: Say it!

JAKE: Give me a fucking bagel!

MATT: You have to say it!

JAKE *(Mimicking Matt exactly)*: Tina Turner Tina Turner Tina Turner.

MATT: Wrong again!

DREW *(In a hungover monotone, making no effort to imitate Matt)*: Tina Turner Tina Turner Tina Turner.

MATT: Correct! Congratulations, Drew.

(Matt gives Drew a bagel.)

JAKE *(Grabbing a bagel from Matt)*: Gimme that, dickhead!

(Jake goes to sit in the easy chair, but Drew jumps into it just as Jake is trying to sit.

Sound of a guitar strum from the hallway. Ed enters singing and playing a guitar badly.

"La la la's" are not pronounced as written, but represent the not-knowing-the-words gibberish noises Ed and his sons come up with as they sing.)

ED:

O Tannenbaum, O Tannenbaum, how are the la la la la.

Everyone!

EVERYONE:

O Tannenbaum, O Tannenbaum, la la la la la la la.
I see the la la la la la.
I got a la la Tannenbaum.

O Tannenbaum, O Tannenbaum.
How are the lovely branches.

(*Matt, Jake and Drew applaud.*)

MATT: That was great, Dad.
JAKE: Very good.

(*Drew goes back to sleep in the easy chair, cuddling his towel.*)

ED (*Taking off his guitar, which Matt takes from him*): I guess
I should have learned the words. And the chords.
JAKE: It's not Christmas anymore, Dad.
ED: I know, but I never got a chance to play for you.
MATT: Dad, you want a bagel?
ED: No, I want cranberry juice with ice!
MATT: Coming right up.
JAKE: No, I'll go.

(*Jake exits. Matt puts away Ed's guitar, then puts* The Birth
of Tragedy *back on the shelf.*
     Ed looks at Drew, who is asleep.)

MATT: I went to the store.
ED: Already? Did you get the steaks?
MATT (*Picking up a wet towel*): Yeah, I got everything. I got stuff
for tomorrow, too.
ED: Oh, what are we having?
MATT: Your favorite, fried chicken.

(*Matt puts the towel in the washing machine.*)

ED: Great! We can invite Mrs. Johnson.
MATT: I thought we could invite Mr. Santana, too.

ED: Is he back at the store?

MATT: Yeah, he looked great.

ED: Oh, I'm glad. That'll be fun.

    Did you get a movie for tonight?

MATT: Yeah, hold on.

(Matt gets a DVD off the mudroom bench and hands it to Ed.)

ED: *A Man for All Seasons!* I haven't seen this in years!

DREW *(Waking up)*: Is that our movie?

ED: Matt got *A Man for All Seasons!*

DREW: I've heard of that.

ED: It's a wonderful film.

JAKE *(Entering with a cranberry juice on ice in an old* Star Wars *Lando Calrissian glass)*: Doesn't sound like an action movie.

MATT: Sorry Jake. You'll like it. It's about divorce.

(Jake mimes strangling Matt.)

DREW: What kind of dick needs ice in December?

(Jake smugly hands the glass to Ed.)

ED: A dick named Dad.

    I'm a dick if I want ice in December?

    It's warm in the house.

JAKE: Is it warm?

ED: What, you're cold?

JAKE: Dad it's freezing in here!

DREW: Is the heat even on?

ED: You know what makes heat? Your bodies. You know what keeps heat close to your bodies? Sweaters.

JAKE: It's ridiculous that we don't turn the heat up! How much more does it cost to live like a human being? Fifty bucks?

ED: I can turn the heat up if you'd all like.

MATT, JAKE AND DREW: Yes!

ED: Yes?

JAKE: Jesus, yeah, it's cold as hell in here!

ED *(Getting up)*: All right. The things I do for you kids.

(He exits.)

JAKE: You think he's really gonna do it?

MATT: I'm skeptical.

DREW: We've kinda got him cornered.

ED *(From the hallway)*: What do you want, eighty?

MATT: Eighty?

ED *(From the hallway)*: Is seventy hot enough? It's at sixty-three right now.

JAKE: Seventy-three.

ED *(From the hallway)*: I'm putting it on seventy.

JAKE: I thought old people were supposed to get cold easily.

MATT: I think saving money is what keeps Dad warm.

(Drew leans forward to reach for a newspaper and Jake shoves him out of the easy chair and jumps into it himself, furiously kicking his legs like he's riding a bicycle, in order to keep Drew from getting back in. Drew goes to sit on the sofa next to Matt, but Matt stretches out his legs to block him.
Ed reenters.)

Since when do you sleep late, Dad?

ED: Oh I wasn't sleeping. I was thinking.

MATT: About what?

ED: I haven't been paying enough attention to your situation.

MATT: What situation?

ED: Your student loans.

MATT: I'm making the payments, Dad. I got it.

ED: Son, those loans are crippling you. You shouldn't have to be stuck here with me.

(Pause.)

Why don't you let me take care of your loans?

MATT: What? Why?

ED: I have the means, and it'll give you the freedom to do whatever you want.

MATT: You should hang on to your money, Dad.

ED: You can think of it as an early inheritance.

MATT: That's really generous, Dad. But you might need it, and I'm okay.

ED: I'm telling you, Matt. I have the means.

MATT: Dad, please.

DREW: Dad, this isn't the kind of problem you can just throw money at.

JAKE: Look Matt, I understand why you wouldn't want to take money from Dad. But you know if you ever needed money . . .

DREW: Matt, I would gladly pay for your therapy!

MATT: Please, guys, stop!

ED: Matt, what is going on?

Are you depressed?

JAKE: He's not depressed!

DREW: Jake, shut up!

JAKE: No! He's feeling exactly the way anyone would feel in his situation!

ED: Boys! Matt, what made you cry at the dinner table?

MATT: I felt like things were weird, and you guys started making a fuss over me.

ED: Matt, you are a person who could be good at anything you wanted.

MATT: No I couldn't, Dad.

ED: Why not?

JAKE: Because—

ED: Jake, hush.

MATT: No one can be good at anything they want.

ED: Well, what's one thing you're not good at?

MATT: I mean, most things.

DREW: Stop putting yourself down!

MATT: What are you talking about? Most people aren't good at most things!

ED: What's one thing you're not good at that prevents you from succeeding?

DREW: Loving himself.

ED: Besides that.

JAKE: Selling himself.

ED: Selling himself? Why does that matter?

JAKE: Today that's all that matters.

ED: What do you mean?

JAKE: Okay. Back in your day, people were all like, "Hey, you got a skill? Great, we'll pay you to use it." Nowadays it doesn't matter if you have any skills or not. You sell yourself, not your skills. But Matt doesn't care about that.

ED: Matt, would you agree that you're not good at selling yourself?

MATT: Probably.

DREW: You don't think you're good at anything!

ED: Drew, enough.

JAKE: He could be good at it if he wanted to, he just doesn't want to!

ED: Why don't you show us?

(Getting up) We'll do an interview!

MATT: What?

ED: A job interview! I'll interview you, and we'll see what the problem is.

(Pause.)

MATT: Okay.

What am I interviewing for?

ED: Well, what sort of job would you like?

MATT: Um . . .

ED: How about policy writing? For a human rights organization.

MATT: It should be an entry-level job.

ED: Okay. How about . . . copyediting for a human rights organization.

MATT: Okay.

ED: Let's see, so come in like this is my office.

(Matt enters the "office.")

(Shaking Matt's hand) Nice to meet you, I'm Ed.

MATT: Matt.

ED: Have a seat.

(Matt sits.)

So Matt, tell me why you're interested in working for our foundation.

MATT: Well, I guess I'm interested in the job because I, uh . . . graded a lot of papers while I was in grad school and . . . um . . . I graded a lot of papers and they were—I have that skill. Which is not to say that I have any of the actual copyediting skills required for this job. But I'm assuming I could learn them if, you know, I was taught.

ED: Good, good. Okay . . .

DREW: Dad, I think you're moving a little fast here. Matt needs to deal with a whole bunch of shit before he can handle something like this.

JAKE: No, he could do it if he wanted. He could do it in his sleep.

DREW: Apparently not.

JAKE: Sure he could!

    (To Matt) Here, I'll show you. Hop up.

    (Matt stands. Jake enters the "office."
    Jake shakes Ed's hand.)

    Hi, I'm Matt.

ED: I'm Ed. Thanks for coming in.

JAKE: No problem. Thanks for having me.

ED: So, Matt, tell me a little about why you're interested in working for our foundation.

JAKE: Well, Sam told me about the position.

ED: Oh, Sam! He spoke very highly of you.

JAKE: Yeah, he's a great friend. We met on our year abroad to Ghana when we were at Harvard.

ED: Ghana! What brought you there?

JAKE: We were part of a project that trained villagers in rural areas to build sustainable housing.

ED: That sounds fascinating.

JAKE: It was amazing to see the difference we were able to make in people's lives. I'm sure you must feel that way all the time.

ED: I certainly do. Matt, your résumé shows a BA from Harvard, ten years in Stanford's PhD program, and ten years at various nonprofits and community organizations. Can you tell me a little about that?

JAKE: Well, for a long time I thought I might stay in academia, but it started to feel too theoretical. I wanted to put some of that theory into action. I worked with a variety of small grassroots organizations in order to learn a wide range of practices, and now I'm ready to bring that knowledge to a larger organization.

ED: Where do you see yourself ten years from now?

JAKE: Well, eventually I'd love to go back to Ghana, and continue my work there as a director of operations.

ED: How wonderful. Well, I must say, Matt, I'm impressed.

It was very nice to meet you. We'll be in touch soon.

JAKE *(Shaking Ed's hand)*: It was great to meet you, too.

ED: Good work, Jake.

JAKE: Thanks, Dad.

ED: See Matt? You've got all the pieces. You've got the résumé. It's just about presentation.

JAKE: I keep telling you, he could do it if he wanted to.

DREW: Not if he has low self-esteem! I know you guys don't want to hear it, but it's the truth! This is sadistic!

ED: Drew, enough with the psychobabble!

Matt, you could be the *director* of a human rights organization.

Did you see what Jake did?

MATT: Yes I did.

ED: Now you try.

MATT: I saw Jake do it, Dad. I got it.

ED: Now I'd like to see *you* try.

JAKE: Just do it and get it over with.

DREW: You don't have to do this, Matt.

(Matt looks at Ed.)

MATT: It's what Dad wants.

(Matt enters the "office.")

ED: Oh, you can't come in like that.

MATT: Like what?

ED: Your shoulders are hunched and you're not making eye contact.

You need to walk in confidently with your head up. Come in again.

MATT: Okay.

(Matt goes out and comes back in.)

ED: Much better! *(Shaking Matt's hand)* Nice to meet you, I'm Ed.

MATT: Matt.

ED: Firm handshake. Very good.

Have a seat.

(They sit.)

So Matt, tell me why you're interested in working for our foundation.

MATT: Uh . . . because . . .

ED: Eye contact, Matt.

MATT: Sam told me about the job.

ED: And how do you know Sam?

MATT: Uh . . . we met at Harvard. No actually, in Ghana. We were both at Harvard at the time, but we were doing our year abroad, so we were in Ghana when we met.

ED: And what were you doing in Ghana?

MATT: Um, well at least in my case, I was teaching a bunch of people something I didn't know how to do, that they didn't want to learn.

ED: Oh come on. I'm sure it wasn't that bad.

MATT: No, I felt like an idiot, and the worst part about it—

ED: Why don't you tell me a little about what you've been doing since you left academia.

MATT: Uh, well . . .

There were things I wasn't smart enough to figure out in academia, so—

ED: How can you say you're not smart?

MATT: It's not that I'm not smart, I'm just not smart enough. I don't know, maybe nobody is.

ED: I'm afraid I don't understand. What were you trying to figure out?

MATT: How to be useful.

(Pause.)

ED: With your education and experience, why haven't you done anything meaningful?

MATT: I don't know . . .

ED: Matt, how can you be this weak in an interview?

DREW: Dad, Matt's interview skills are not the problem!

   (To Matt) You're trapped in a sick way of thinking!

MATT: Drew, stop helping! You're not good at it.

DREW: Wait a minute, wait a minute! I've just been sitting here! I've barely said anything!

MATT: You keep insisting something's wrong with me!

DREW: Because I care about you!

MATT: I'm just trying to be useful! That's it! What's wrong with that?

DREW: You're not happy! Why don't you want that?

MATT: Honestly, Drew, everything was fine before you guys got here!

DREW: So you were loving doing temp work?

MATT: It's a decent organization! And someone has to do what they have me doing!

DREW: And you want to keep doing that forever?

MATT: I can't do it forever! It's a temp job!

DREW: Jesus, nothing escapes the vortex of negativity!

JAKE: He just said he feels good about what he's doing!

DREW: That's not possible!

JAKE: Yes it is! Why don't you get it? All our lives, guys like us have been told to get out of the way so that other people can have a chance. Matt's actually doing what they want! It's noble!

MATT: I'm not being noble!

JAKE: Yes you are! You're making copies for the oppressed! You just don't feel noble because no one appreciates it. All your minority co-workers are probably too busy with their ambition to notice you're there.

ED: Jake, you believe that Matt is trying to make the world better by sabotaging himself?

JAKE: Yes!

ED: I don't buy it.

JAKE: That's because nobody else would ever do it! Matt's a freak.

ED: Jake!

JAKE: I mean that as a compliment.

It's a world of pigs, and Matt is not a pig! But if you're not a pig, you're fucked!

Look at me! I'm an asshole, but people kind of like me, whether they know it or not.

DREW: Jake, you're not as big an asshole as you'd like to think.

JAKE: Yes, I am!

I give my friends shit for acting "gay." I joke about which interns I want to fuck.

DREW: The horror.

JAKE: No, listen to me. Every single VP at my company is white. Minorities don't climb the ladder, at all. There are so many talented women and people of color in the office that I'd love to bring to client meetings, but I only bring white guys because that's how the clients want it. I'm excluding Black people at work, even though my kids are half Black!

All day long, I reinforce a system that keeps us on top. But Matt's doing the opposite! He's making his way to the bottom. He's being a martyr!

MATT: I'm not a martyr!

JAKE: Are you kidding me? Come on!

DREW: If Matt is trying to fight the system by martyring himself, then he has serious issues.

JAKE: Drew, stop being an idiot.

DREW: You're the idiot! You're trying to paint Matt as some big hero, but you're full of shit! What if Miles decided he wanted to be a hero just like his Uncle Matt? Or Olivia? What if they were like, "Oh, it's so unfair that we're rich kids! We're gonna do nothing with our lives so that poor kids can have a chance!"

(Jake doesn't respond.)

Yeah! You would lose your shit!

If you truly admired what Matt was doing, you'd be doing it yourself, but you're not! You're a rich banker who's not doing shit! You're actively making things worse!

JAKE: Yeah, I know.

DREW: He probably needs medication!

ED: Okay, can we please stop talking about Matt like he's not in the room?

Matt, you can speak for yourself.

MATT: I don't believe the things you all think I believe!

JAKE: So what do you believe?

MATT: I don't know! I don't know anything!

JAKE: So you don't even have your principles? You're a loser for no reason?

ED: Hey!

JAKE: Hang on, answer my question! Are you a loser for no reason?

MATT: If you say so.

JAKE: Then you might as well be dead!

ED: Jake, stop.

JAKE: What? Matt, for the past three days, I've been defending you and fucking looking up to you for having the courage of your convictions. It made me feel horrible about myself, but it made me feel better about everything else. Then it turns out you're not doing anything? You're just . . . giving in to the total hopelessness of everything, being a loser for no reason?

DREW: Jake.

JAKE: Drew's right! I'd be appalled if Olivia or Miles wasted their talent for no reason whatsoever!

So what, you're a poor little white boy who doesn't want to take a check from his daddy? You're a poor little white boy who doesn't want to use his degrees? Who fucking cares about that kind of loser?

DREW: Jake, stop.

(Drew touches Jake.)

JAKE: Get the fuck off me!

Matt, are you quitting? Are you giving up?

MATT: If you say so.

*(Jake grabs Matt and grapples with him.
Drew pulls Jake off Matt.)*

DREW: Hey, stop!

(Jake stares at Matt, then exits.)

Are you okay?

MATT *(Walking away)*: Yeah, I'm fine.

(Drew follows him.)

DREW: Matt, come on, just wait a second. Matt, please!

(Matt stops.)

Can't you see what it's doing to us to see you like this?
MATT: Like what?
DREW: Like, this tragic, fucking, just . . . nonentity!

(Matt moves away again.)

That came out wrong! That came out wrong!
Please, hear me out.

(Matt stops.)

I just . . . Matt, do you remember when I went through that big depression in grad school where I was like, fucking suicidal?
MATT: Yeah.
DREW: I remember calling you, and you convincing me to take a shower. And then four hours later, once I'd managed to do that, you talked me into eating a sandwich. And little by little, step by step, you got me through the worst of it. I don't know how I would have survived that time without you.

But that's all I was doing, was surviving. I wasn't really living. So then Mom died . . . and I went to see a therapist, and my whole fucking life started to change. Every good thing that's happened to me has happened since then! Matt, please just give it a shot!
MATT: Drew, I'm okay.

DREW: So you want to keep going like this? You don't want anything better? You don't want a career?

MATT: No.

DREW: Is it because you think you don't deserve one?

MATT: No! Why do I have to have a career?

DREW: Okay, fuck a career. What if I found you a therapist who would do it pro bono?

MATT: I don't think it's a good idea.

DREW: Why not?

MATT: It would be very unpleasant for me.

DREW: Okay. Why?

MATT: Well, wouldn't it be kind of like this conversation we're having now?

DREW: Matt, you gotta help me out here. I'm not gonna watch you destroy your life. I've been enabling you for too long. I'm not gonna do it.

    If you won't agree to make some honest attempt to improve your life, I'm done, man. I can't have any more contact with you.

MATT: Drew, please.

DREW: NO, NO, NO, NO!

    Just promise me you're gonna take one positive step. I'll do everything in my power to help you.

MATT: I can't do that.

DREW: You would choose staying in this situation over having a relationship with me?

(Pause. Matt doesn't respond.)

Okay. Enjoy your misery.

(Drew exits.
    Pause.
    Ed comes over to Matt.)

ED: Matt, here's what we need to do.

(Ed takes out a check and puts it in front of Matt.)

You're gonna take this and pay off your loans.
　　You have so much potential.

MATT: I can't take your money, Dad.

ED: Yes you can.

MATT: I didn't earn it.

ED: What does it matter if you earned the money or not? Take the check.

MATT: I don't want it!

ED: Matt, what is wrong with you?

MATT: Nothing's wrong, Dad! For the first time in a long time, I don't feel bad about what I'm doing! I feel useful!

ED: But what you're doing isn't actually useful. Especially considering everything that's been invested in you. You should be doing more than cooking and cleaning like a housemaid!

MATT: I want to be here.

ED: It's repugnant, Matt. There's something repugnant about it.
　　I wonder what your mother would say if she were here.

(Pause.)

MATT: She would tell me to take a walk every day around the lake, and to fix her garden.
　　She would say there's nothing you can do to erase the problem of your own existence. She would tell me to not despair, and to keep trying to find my way.

ED: That's what I keep trying to say!

MATT: No, it isn't.

ED: Your mother would have wanted you out there making the world a better place.

MATT: I spent my whole life trying to make things better, and everything I did just made things worse!

ED: Because white guys can't do anything right?

MATT: No, Dad! Nobody has the answers! I don't know if there is an answer!

ED: I love you so much. I've never done anything but love you.

I look at you now and don't even recognize you.

I feel like I haven't done a good job as a father.

(Matt puts his hand on Ed's knee. Ed puts his hand over Matt's and removes Matt's hand from his knee.)

I won't be your excuse. I can't have you staying here anymore.

MATT: Dad—

ED *(Getting up)*: This is for your own good.

(Ed walks away. He stops and turns.)

I love you, pal, but I'm sorry.

(Ed exits.

Matt sits alone.

Matt looks up and out.

The People in Charge enter and look at him. They look at each other. Person in Charge 2 snaps their fingers to cue the:

Blackout.)

END

www.nickhernbooks.co.uk

facebook.com/nickhernbooks

twitter.com/nickhernbooks